The Hyphenated American

Also by the author

Porcelain

A Language of Their Own

The Hyphenated American
Four Plays by Chay Yew

Red
Scissors
A Beautiful Country
Wonderland

Foreword by
Craig Lucas
Introduction by
David Román

Grove Press
New York

Published simultaneously in Canada
Printed in the United States of America

FIRST EDITION

Library of Congress Cataloging-in-Publication Data
Yew, Chay.
    The hyphenated American : four plays / by Chay Yew ; foreword by Craig Lucas ;
introduction by David Román.—1st ed.
        p. cm.
    Contents: Red — Scissors — A beautiful country — Wonderland.
    ISBN 0-8021-3912-4
        1. Asian Americans—Drama. I. Title.
PS3575.E9 H96 2002
822'.54—dc21   2002027114

Grove Press
841 Broadway
New York, NY 10003

02 03 04 05 10 9 8 7 6 5 4 3 2 1

For My Parents

who let me

come to the

Beautiful Country

CONTENTS

Foreword

You can have a play without scenery. You can have a play without expensive costumes or special lights, without music and projections and video screens. You cannot have a play without actors.

Actors and a story.

If you take away all the special effects in a movie, all the close-ups, the long shots, tracking shots, the music and editing, take away the camera and the film, then and only then can you begin to approach the power of theater—what it's like to be on a movie set watching the performers right in front of you, not looking through the lens. Our eyes already have lenses. Our ears already have sound equipment. Our concentration is the most sophisticated editing machine on the planet: Look here! Now look over here! Why would we want someone to do all that work for us? Can we become any less alive?

Chay Yew knows all this in his bones. How you have to be there. Really be there. What could be more transporting than a man, a woman, a young man, standing before us enacting the story of a family—playing all the parts, assuming new shapes, new perspectives, nationalities, histories, desires, secrets. What do you have? *Wonderland*. Chay Yew treats the audience to the wonderland that is the shifting ground of being alive, reinvented for the darkness of theater. It's a paradox: we sit in the dark in order to be illuminated. No character is to be trusted, nor are they ever to be diminished by judgment. All things are possible and nothing is certain. Things change.

Another unique property of theater is its ability to take us places without literally showing it to us—everything is by inference, suggestion. (Plays on TV are not plays, they're TV. Plays that take to TV like a duck to water were already TV, at least in part.) We must put the pieces of the puzzle together ourselves. Who are

ix

these two men in Chinatown, sharing a haircut? The play doesn't tell us, it shows us their separate perspectives, even though one of them is blind. The blind man can see as much as the seeing man if he knows how to listen and pay attention to the details.

The meaning of the Cultural Revolution in the lives of three individuals who do not fit anyone's preconceived idea of what makes an artist, a journalist, a student, a pawn in a terrifying game outside of one's control—these things are not easily captured, they must be teased out of behavior, behavior, behavior. And one must know how to look and to listen.

Chay Yew knows how to look, listen, and even more thrillingly, how to tease us into doing the same for ourselves. No two audience members can have the same experience of any of these remarkably different plays (and I mean different from each other as well as from the wide and banal landscape of most English-language theater today), because the plays do not tell you what to feel or think. The violin music is never present, even in the most poignant moment. Listen: the air is clear. One can always step back and think, or lean forward and get lost. It's up to you, it hasn't already been decided upon. The string section is inside you. Or not.

These plays are why I wanted to be in the theater.

Craig Lucas
New York

INTRODUCTION

The four plays collected in this remarkable volume demonstrate why Chay Yew, a Los Angeles–based playwright, is at the forefront of American theater. Chay Yew's theater brings to the foreground the lives and experiences of those he calls the "hyphenated American," people who live at the intersection of multiple and overlapping worlds: Asia and America, citizenship and exile, migration and home. The hyphenated American also describes those for whom the nomenclature "American" needs to be further marked by yet another term. In most cases in Yew's world this other term is "Asian." While an earlier generation of Asian-American playwrights, artists, and activists felt it necessary to name themselves and their work and movement "Asian-American," Yew feels it necessary to call the stability of "Asian-American" itself into question. Yew's theater sets out to unsettle our comfort with the normative world of Asian-America. He writes plays that while informed by the traditions of Asian-American theater, set out to move that tradition forward. "It's your turn now, go make history," an elder character tells a younger one in *Red,* one of the plays published in this volume, in an emotionally charged scene marking the shift from one generation to another. *The Hyphenated American* captures this sense of history in the making; it is a dynamic collection of plays showcasing the dramaturgical versatility of Chay Yew's theatrical vision.

Chay Yew is the generational and artistic heir to such prominent Asian-American playwrights as Philip Kan Gotanda, David Henry Hwang, and Velina Hausa Houston whose work began appearing in the early 1980s. These important and still relevant foundational writers, often named "first generation" Asian-American playwrights, provided the vocabulary for self representations of Asian-American experience on stage and thereby helped shape the political and artistic space within which Yew's work would later emerge. He no longer carries the burden of representation that these earlier playwrights faced. Yew's work is less bound to positive images of Asian-Americans and less interested in explaining what it means to be "Asian-American" to others. In this sense, it is important to note that Yew is also the generational peer of midcareer playwrights such as Suzan-Lori Parks and José Rivera whose interest in artistic innovation and formal experimentation departs from traditional realist forms. These playwrights are also "hyphenated Americans" in that they emerge from particular U.S. racial and cultural minorities. But it would be a mistake to think that their dramaturgy only ruptures traditional ideas of African-American theater, Latino theater, or Asian-American theater. These playwrights challenge us to reimagine American theater, and by extension, American culture. In other words, the hyphen works on the terms on both of its sides. In Yew's plays, for example, we are asked to rethink not simply what is "Asian-American" but more broadly what might constitute "American."

In *Red,* for example, the protagonist Sonja Wong Pickford, an established and immensely successful writer of ethnic romance fiction, decides to return to the China of her youth in order to break out of a pattern of predictability and write something new, something with more weight and importance. Rather than re-circulate yet another set of Orientalist tropes for her both white and Asian-American audiences, Sonja decides to embark on a creative journey that will transform her sense of self. Sonja's success in America might stand in for the success of an earlier model of Asian-American experience. But rather than dwell on how Sonja has maneuvered through American culture, Yew brackets her narrative of migration and exile to tell the story of Master Hua, a star of the Beijing Opera, who during Mao's Cultural Revolution fought to preserve his theater and his art form. Amidst a climate of cultural suppression and censorship, Hua's efforts to sustain the traditions of a historic but fragile cultural practice remind Sonja of the serious political stakes involved in artistic practice. Sonja's interest in Hua's story is shaped by an increasing need for her to come to terms with her past. Sonja's journey from China to Hong Kong to America and then back to China is haunted by a troubled history of political and personal betrayals. Written in response to the U.S. culture wars of the late 1980s and early 1990s, *Red* asks us to consider the role of the arts in our own society. What is the function of art in a time of cultural conservatism? Are the arts primarily a means of entertainment and leisure or might they help us to imagine and articulate a more just world? *Red,* which is framed by Sonja's perspective, asks its audiences to attend to the lessons of history and the role of the artist to shape history.

Scissors, Yew's exquisite short one-act play about two characters living through the Great Depression of the 1930s, cuts through the racial barriers that keep white and Asian America separate. Set in New York immediately after the crash of the stock market, *Scissors* concerns two older men, one "Asian" and one "American," who meet for a ritual haircut. Yew fleshes out the often-demeaning trope of the Asian worker who must serve the white master—"the Asian houseboy" stereotype—so that the connection between these men becomes profound and lasting. The two characters, named A and B to signal that the play will not dwell on their personal pasts, but rather rely on their own shared history of friendship and their ritual of the scissors to preserve the dignity of their lives. This intragenerational alliance is in stark contrast to the intergenerational tension between parents and children. The economy of the dialogue between these two men calls attention to the possibility of friendship and community across racial identities. Despite intensifying economic constraints and sustained inequities of power, A and B are able to forge ahead together through mutual affection and respect.

A Beautiful Country is a collaboration between Chay Yew and Cornerstone Theater, a Los Angeles–based company that according to its mission, "builds bridges between and within diverse communities." The play recovers a history of Asian-American immigrant experience through dance and drama. *A Beautiful County* chronicles a 150-year history of Pan-Asian immigration and exile to the United States; from Filipino migrant workers in the 1930s to Hmong refugees in the 1970s and 1980s; from the effects of the 1882 Chinese Exclusion Acts to the internment of Japanese-Americans during World War II; from the Negro Alley Massacre in Los Angeles in 1885, where fifteen Chinese men were hanged and four others were shot and stabbed to death during an interracial riot; to recent hate crimes against new Asian immigrants. A multiracial cast, composed of professional actors and community members from the Chinatown neighborhood where the play was presented, performed these stories. *A Beautiful Country* is neither a chronological history play nor a docudrama of Asian-American history. Rather, Yew stages the various contradictions of Pan-Asian American experience, the ways in which racial and national identities are historically constructed. At the heart of the play is the character Miss Visa Denied, a Malaysian drag queen searching for a sense of identity and home. Visa, much like *Red*'s Sonja Wong Pickford, must negotiate the hyphen and work against a cultural logic that positions her as foreign in both Asia and America. After a lifetime framed by the question "Stay or go? Stay or go?" Visa finds respite in Los Angeles. Visa's final triumph is a tribute to the historical and political legacy of Asian-Americans in the United States and *A Beautiful Country* is Yew's celebration of this achievement.

Visa's queerness adds a distinctive and theatrical twist to *A Beautiful Country* and marks Yew's continuing interest in writing about queer sexuality in Asian-American communities. This theme was introduced in *Porcelain* and *A Language of Their Own,* two earlier plays from Yew's career that have been previously published by Grove Press. The final play in this collection, *Wonderland,* was initially written as the last play of a trilogy that began with these earlier works. The trilogy highlights the lives and experiences of queer Asian-Americans and provided one of the first sustained explorations of this theme in American literature. *Wonderland* focuses on a family of three—man, woman, son—who buy into the promise of America only to find themselves destroyed by it. Through a stunning series of moving and poetic soliloquies that help structure the play, we learn of their dreams and aspirations and of their efforts to survive amidst the increasing pressures of life in America. The man, an architect interested in designing "monuments, skyscrapers, concert halls," instead finds himself building suburban strip malls with impatience and growing apathy. The woman, an ambitious and idealistic new immigrant whose sense of America is disproportionately informed by the films of Elizabeth Taylor, finds herself by the end of the play identifying more with an earlier casualty of Southern California, the imperial mammoths of the La Brea Tar Pits. The son, an adventurous gay teenager, grows increasingly alienated from both of these disconnected parents and finds an alternative home in Hollywood's subcultural world of drugs, pornography, and the sex industry. Each of these characters must "run far, run free" in an effort to escape the constraints of an increasingly tragic world. "She crossed her ocean, and you crossed yours," the son acknowledges of the woman in a moment of heartbreaking epiphany. Like most of Yew's characters, these are people on the move from place to place, sometimes by choice and sometimes not, searching for a sense of home and identity often against the odds. The costs of their migrations are many, all testaments to what we must do to survive in the wonderland we call America.

These are brave and beautiful plays that have moved multiple audiences both in the United States and abroad. I have been fortunate to have seen these productions throughout these past years in Los Angeles, New York City, and Seattle in some of the most accomplished regional theaters in the United States. Each time I am in Yew's audience, I am impressed by the extraordinary care of his writing and the innovative theatricality of his plays. Yew's plays are striking both in their poetics and in the audacity of their critique of Asian and American culture. He also has a wicked sense of humor that undercuts the solemnity of some of his themes. This combination of irony and insight, camp and profundity makes reading the plays highly enjoyable. *The Hyphenated American* is an extraordinary achievement by one of America's most gifted playwrights.

David Román
University of Southern California
Los Angeles

ACKNOWLEDGMENTS

The playwright wishes to thank the following remarkable artists and individuals who made these plays a reality:

Luis Alfaro, Tim Dang, Gordon Davidson, Sonja Dosti, Robert Egan, Morgan Jenness, Tod London, Jon Nakagawa, Ben Pesner, Lisa Peterson, Diane Rodriguez, David Román, Theatre Communications Group/Pew Charitable Trusts' National Theatre Artists Residency Program, Alice Tuan, and Annie Weisman for their unwavering support, encouragement and friendship throughout the process.

John Buzzetti for always being there.

Liz Engelman, Warner Shook, and the Intiman Theatre; Elizabeth Huddle and Portland Center Stage; Doug Hughes, Greg Leaming, and the Long Wharf Theater; Lynne Meadow, Christian Parker, and the Manhattan Theatre Club; Mead Hunter, and A.S.K. Theater Projects; Shelby Jiggetts, George C. Wolfe, and the Public Theater; Gaurav Kripalani and Singapore Repertory Theatre; East West Players; Paul Willis and Printers' Devil Theater; Kate Loewald; and David Petrarca for *Red*.

Michael Greif, Neel Keller, Elizabeth Bennett, and La Jolla Playhouse; Linda Chapman, Jim Nicola, and New York Theatre Workshop; Mark Taper Forum's New Works Festival; and East West Players for *Wonderland*.

Bill Rauch, Leslie Tamarabuchi, Los Angeles' Chinatown, and Cornerstone Theater Company; and Judith Nihei and Northwest Asian American Theatre for *A Beautiful Country*.

Mark Taper Forum, East West Players, New Dramatists, and Northwest Asian American Theatre for giving me an artistic home to call my own.

RED

(from left to right) Emily Kuroda (Sonja Wong Pickford), Jeanne Sakata (Hua), and Page Leong (Ling). Photo: Michael Lamont

Red was first presented in Seattle on August 28, 1998, by the Intiman Theater; Warner Shook, artistic director.

Sonja	Jeanne Sakata
Hua	Sab Shimono
Ling	Michi Barall
Director	Lisa Peterson
Set Design	Rachel Hauck
Costume Design	Michael Olich
Lighting Design	Mary Louise Geiger
Original Music and Sound Design	Nathan Wang
Choreographer	Jamie H. J. Guan
Dramaturge	Steven Alter
Production Stage Manager	Lisa Loeb

This version of *Red* was presented in Singapore on June 21, 2001, by Singapore Repertory Theatre, Gaurav Kripalani, artistic director. The production transferred to Los Angeles on September 27, 2001 at East West Players; Tim Dang, artistic director.

Sonja	Emily Kuroda
Hua	Jeanne Sakata
Ling	Page Leong
Director	Chay Yew
Set Design	Myung Hee Cho
Costume Design	Anita Yavich
Lighting Design	José Lopez
Original Music and Sound Design	Nathan Wang
Choreography	Dr. Chua Soo Pong, Madam Li Xiu Hua
Production Stage Managers	Kyle Rudgers, Victoria Gathe

Red was originally commissioned
by the New York Shakespeare Festival.

Red is for Tsai Chin.

RED

Upstage is a cyclorama.

In the center of the stage, there is a wooden platform where all the action of the play is performed.

Upstage is a passageway between the platform and the cyclorama where scenes can also be played.

The main idea is to keep the production simple and theatrical suggestion is key. Hence, a chair can be used to suggest a dressing table; actors can mime putting on makeup.

On the side of the stage are about five wooden chairs on each side. The stagehands will sit in these chairs and hand out the appropriate props to the actors; actors can also sit on these chairs if they are acting in their scenes.

The stagehands will also use the chairs to create sound effects.

Fluidity between scenes is key. Musical transitions can be used.

PROLOGUE

SONJA *enters the front of the house and speaks to the audience.*

SONJA   Story of my life.

There I was,
at the height of my career,
swimming in a dizzying swamp
of parties, paparazzi,
press, and personalities.

I'm an author.
Sonja Wong Pickford.

You may have heard of me.
Love in the Jade Pagoda?
Bound Feet, Bound Lives?

If some of you haven't,
visit your local bookstore,
look under "romance,"
and there I am

After twenty years
in the business,
I grew tired
of churning out characters,
stories I didn't care for.

Nothing spoke to me.
Nothing moved me.

Truth be told,
I was also afraid to die,
and leave behind
a legacy of ethnic romances
to my name.

With the deadline of my next book
looming around the corner,
I thought
I'd write something more
than my usual fare.
Something important.
Something big.
Something credible.

But
nothing came to me.

So
I took a trip to China.

I thought
a change of environment,
of air,
may just be the right thing.

Lights change to indicate that Sonja is in China. She walks to the other side of the front of house.

SONJA   On my first day there,
I took to wandering
the streets of Shanghai.

Feeling tired
from an entire day,
immersing in a noisy ocean
of street pedestrians,
buzzing cars
whizzing bicycles,
I sought refuge
walking on the smaller,
quieter, untraveled side streets.

In one particular alley,
I suddenly
came across
an opera theatre.

Sonja turns and looks up on stage. Sonja sees a mass of chairs strewn about on stage.

SONJA   Old,
yet strangely familiar,
the theatre flooded me
with a curious sense of déjà vu.
A dignified building,
unimposing,

7

it was tucked away
amongst the taller,
newer, grayer monstrosities
in which the Chinese now live.

(Climbs on stage and onto the platform)

It was derelict,
abandoned,
silent.

Its terra-cotta roof
left mostly unshingled.
A red Communist flag
fluttering defiantly
on the very same roof.

(Gestures with her hands as if opening a door)

When I shoved the doors open,
I was immediately assaulted.
A sharp stab of mold
in the dank air.

Upon careful scrutiny
I found broken, deflated red lanterns
resting on dirt floors.

Next to the lanterns were
riveting embroidered pictures of
blazing phoenixes,
fiery dragons,
in fight,
in flight,
adorning silk stage curtains
that were once found hanging
in front of the proscenium,

a grand welcome,
to visitors of this inner sanctum.

The walls,
you could tell,
were once
brightly and opulently
painted
in majestic gold.

Now
they peeled
like dull moths.

I got up
on the dilapidated stage.

Stared into
the silent sea
of broken chairs
where people once sat.

I've never felt
more alone
in my life.

(*Walks to another part of the stage*)

Then I made my way
back stage.

There,
I found a dressing table
covered by
a gentle carpet of dust.

Sonja rests her head on the table.

9

Sounds of applause.

HUA *enters.*

When he sees Sonja resting her head on the dressing table, he claps his hands loudly.

Sonja wakes up in a start.

SONJA   Excuse me—
        I didn't think anyone was—

Sonja stands up. Hua sits down at the table. Sonja glares at Hua.

HUA   Tourist?

SONJA   No—
        not really—
        I'm

HUA   Tours to the theatre were at three—
      you're late—

SONJA   I thought
        this theatre was abandoned and—

HUA   Are you a fan?

SONJA   No—

HUA   I am not receiving any fans today.

SONJA   I know you–

HUA   Many do—

SONJA   You are–

Sonja struggles to remember. Hua glares at Sonja.

HUA   Master Hua—

SONJA Yes—Hua Wai Mun—

HUA The famous opera star—

SONJA I thought you were—

HUA Now that I've satisfied your curiosity,
please leave.

Silence.

Sonja stands staring at Hua.

HUA Why are you still here?

SONJA Do you know who I am?

HUA Must I?

SONJA I'm—Sonja Wong Pickford.

HUA You are in my way.
I have an entrance to make.

Hua gets up and walks to the wings.

Music transition.

2.

On stage.

*Sonja stands unobtrusively at the corner of the stage observing the
following scene.*

Sonja enters every LING *and Hua scene throughout the play as a
silent observer.*

*Hua sings an aria. With grace and beauty, he croons the aria with
delight, precision, and passion.*

HUA   "I flee
       from the valley of my home
       my world
       my life

       I flee
       toward mountains of uncertainty

       I wonder
       if I will again be home

       I wonder
       which path will lead me home"

At the most climatic moment of his song, Ling, wearing a Red Guard uniform, bursts into the house.

LING   You!

Hua keeps singing.

LING   Hey you!
       Stop singing at once!
       Come down from there!

       Do you hear me?

       Stop singing filth
       on the People's stage!

Hua glares at Ling and deliberately ignores her. He keeps singing.

LING   Are you listening?
       You dare sing such nonsense!

       Come down at once!
       Come down now!

Hua continues to sing louder and more histrionically.

LING   What you are singing is
       counterrevolutionary!

Ling bolts up onto the stage and stands beside him. She sings a revolutionary song loudly, drowning Hua out.

LING   "Our red flag flies
defiant in the sky!

Our red army
will expand!

On blue-collared comrades
we'll depend!

Our red country
we'll defend!"

Both Hua and Ling compete with each other. The orchestra stops playing.

Finally, a glaring Hua gives up and leaves in a huff.

Looking at him, Ling continues to sing in triumph.

3.

Back stage.

From the previous scene, Hua enters and goes to the dressing table. He takes off his costume and makeup.

HUA   You!

Don't just stand there
like a blinking fool!

Alert Stage Manager Kong.
Tell him never to let
those Red Guard hooligans
into my theater again!

They disrupt my performance!

Hua tosses his costume to Sonja.

HUA Here!

Have them cleaned and pressed
by tomorrow afternoon.
The way I like it.

And where's my tea?

Hua exits in a huff.

4.

On stage.

Hua stands on a chair. As a punishment, he is holding the same opera costume, from the last scene, with his outstretched arms.

Ling paces the stage.

HUA "I wonder
if I will again
be home

I wonder
which path
will lead me home"

Pause.

LING (*Sweetly*) Sing.
Again.

This time,
with more feeling.

HUA I can't anymore.

LING Try.
The last time—
was just lovely—

HUA Please—

LING Please, Comrade Ling.

Beat.

HUA Please, Comrade Ling,

I can't anymore.

LING Isn't this the same theater,
the same stage,
where you've always graced
the good people of China
with your little songs?

Surely,
you cannot deprive us
of your theatrical gifts now, Comrade Hua.

You have a responsibility.

Come on.
Sing.
For the people.
For the esteemed Chairman.

HUA But
there's no one here in the theater!
I sing for audiences,
not for empty—

LING Pretend it's a rehearsal—

15

HUA   I'm tired.

LING   Sing!

Hua sings in a hoarse and beaten voice.

HUA   "I flee
from the—"

LING   That's not good enough!
You must put some heart into it.

Sing.
From the beginning.

HUA   But
I've sung this aria
more than twenty times today.

LING   And I like it
every time I hear it.

HUA   I can't anymore,
please, Comrade Ling.

LING   You can.

HUA   I said
I can't.

LING   And I said you can.

HUA   I'm exhausted.

LING   You have to *ren*.

Hua glares at Ling.

HUA   *Ren.*

LING   Yes.
Ren.

You have to endure.

The aria is so beautiful.

When does
the White-Haired Damsel
sing it?

HUA I don't remember.

LING I do.

Just after
she's been brutally raped
by the evil landlord,
she sings it,
while escaping
into the dark cold mountains.
Heartbreaking.

Oh and
throw some of your acting
into the song.

Again.
Sing.

HUA No.

Hua gets off the chair.

LING Sing!

Hua stands glaring at Ling.

HUA No.

LING Sing!

Ling slaps Hua across the face.

LING (*Softly*)   Sing.

Beat.

Ling slaps Hua across the face.

LING   Sing.

Beat.

Ling slaps Hua across the face.

LING   Sing.

Hua falls to the ground. He sings a quiet and beautiful aria. Ling hauls Hua off the ground and throws the costume back into his arms.

HUA   "I flee
from the valley of my home
my world
my life—"

Ling throws her head back, closes her eyes.

LING   Beautiful.
Simply beautiful.

5.

Back stage.

From the previous scene, Hua enters and goes to his dressing table.

HUA   Why are you still here?
Go away.

SONJA   Are you all right?

HUA   I'm in pain.
What do you want?

SONJA   I would like to speak to you.

HUA   I can't speak
to any more government officials.
Interrogate me tomorrow.
I need my rest.

Hua points off stage.

HUA   See?
The door over there?
Use it.

SONJA   I'm not from the government.

HUA   Who are you then?

SONJA   I'm a writer.

HUA   I don't make a habit
of speaking to journalists.
Leave me.

SONJA   Not a journalist.
An author.

HUA   Books?

SONJA   Books.

Hua looks at Sonja for the first time.

HUA   An artist.

SONJA   I guess so.

HUA   There are no "guess so's"
in what we do.

You are either
an artist
or you're not.

Don't waste my time.

SONJA (*Hesitantly*) Yes.
I am.
An artist.

HUA My robe.
Over there.
By the screens.

Hua points off stage.

HUA So
you are a writer.

SONJA Yes.

HUA So
tell me.
What subjects?
Your books?

SONJA Romance.

HUA I guess
we all have to make a living.

Sonja retrieves Hua's robe and hands it to him. Hua doesn't take the robe. Instead, he stretches his arms out. A beat later, Sonja helps Hua into his robe.

SONJA I know what you are thinking.

Most of my novels
topped the
New York Times Best–Sellers List.

Translated into
twenty languages around the world.

Some of them were made into TV movies.

Bound Feet, Bound Lives.
Love in the Jade Pagoda.

People consider me to be
the Asian Danielle Steel.

HUA Why do you want to speak to me?

SONJA I am not sure—

Hua studies Sonja for a moment.

HUA You want to write a book about me!

SONJA No—

HUA Admit it!
I see through your ruse—

SONJA I'm sure it's a great idea—

HUA It's a wonderful idea.

A book.
About me.

High time!

SONJA I didn't say—

HUA A book about my career.
My influence on theater and artists.
My success, my fans, my life.

Yes.
I think
I make a very interesting subject.

Sonja thinks hard.

SONJA Yes.

HUA What title are you giving my book?

SONJA I don't—

HUA How about—
Hua Wai Mun: The Legend, The Star, The Man?

SONJA It is a good idea—

HUA Fiction or fact?

SONJA I'm not sure yet.

HUA Fact!

Will there be photographs?
I have tons.

Hua rummages through his dressing table drawer.

SONJA I can start by asking some questions—

Hua fishes out a photograph and hands it to Sonja.

HUA Here.

SONJA I recognize this—

HUA This is a picture of me—

SONJA Yes—

HUA In the early days.
Me in Russia.
With Bertolt Brecht.

SONJA Who?

HUA I'm the one in the dress.

SONJA Pretty.

HUA Come back tomorrow.

SONJA But—

HUA   It's late.

Besides
I have to learn some lines
for tomorrow's performance.

SONJA   A new opera?

HUA   You could say that.

Hua takes out a little red book.

HUA (*Smiles*)   Chairman Mao's teachings.

6.

On stage.

Hua kneels in front of Ling. Ling sits facing him.

LING   Confess!

HUA   I have nothing to confess.

LING   Confess
you use your little romantic operas
to subvert and pollute the masses.

HUA   You give me
far too much credit, Comrade Ling.

LING   You are not my comrade.
You are a class enemy—

Hua takes out the little red book and opens to a specific page. Hua shows the page to Ling.

HUA   Comrade Ling,
didn't our great leader Chairman Mao
teach us:

"Lay out the facts
and speak with reason?"
I have only spoken the truth.

Ling grabs the little red book from Hua.

LING   The great word of our leader
has nothing to do
with the likes of you.

HUA   Set up an investigation.
Check all the facts I've told you.
You will see that I'm not guilty.

LING   Comrade Hua,
do you know of a man who
works under your employ?
Tall and wiry
with the same annoying high-pitched
effeminate voice like yours?
Stage Manager Kong?

HUA   Yes.

LING   Before the crowds and the tribunal yesterday,
Stage Manager Kong,
he delivered a most damaging testimony
against you—

HUA   Fabrication!
It was false testimony—
you and your lackeys coerced him—

LING   Stage Manger Kong's testimony states
and I quote—
"he uses his art
as a weapon

for counterrevolutionary propaganda
to sway the masses
to his perverse thinking."

HUA His vocabulary is not large enough
to say what you have parroted.
Stage Manager Kong could never say—

LING "He puts on female clothing.
Struts on stage.
Thinks he is a grand old lady."

HUA I play woman warriors.
Not old ladies.

And I don't strut.

*Ling spits at Hua. Ling walks away from him and starts burning
books and papers in a metal bin.*

HUA Actually, Comrade Ling,
I'm truly surprised
to hear your resentment
toward theater artists.

Hua wipes off the spit on his face.

HUA Surely
you knew our great leader Chairman Mao
deployed me to the countryside
to spread his word,
his teachings?

LING What word,
what teachings?
Lies!

Why would Chairman Mao do such a thing?

HUA   Who do you think
sang operas
to the tired hungry disenchanted
farmers and peasants
in the early days of Communism?

Who do you think
opened their eyes
to the oppression they suffered
under the evil nationalists
and imperialists?

Who?

We artists.
That's who.

I was the Chairman's messenger.

And yes,
dressed in a brocade gown!

LING   Lies!

HUA   We artists
are the true foot soldiers
of the motherland!

LING   Rubbish!

HUA   You don't even know that,
do you?
You and your Red Guards
don't even know your history!
How can you
expect to make history
without learning it,
without understanding it?

So
you reinvent your history.
Wipe the slate clean.

Anything you don't want to learn,
into the fire.
Anything that makes you uncomfortable,
into the fire.

With your so-called Cultural Revolution,
you and your arrogant Red Guards
overthrew our schools,
expelled our teachers.
Ransacked our country
of our art,
our literature.
Discarded
everything that was of value,
of worth.
Destroyed
everything that made our country great.

Anything and everything,
into the fire.

Ling deliberately grabs an opera costume and aims to throw it into the bin. Hua gets up from his knees and rushes to Ling. Hua wrestles the costume out of Ling's hands. Ling doesn't look at Hua. Ling holds out her hands.

Long silence.

Hua unwillingly puts the costume into Ling's hands. Ling forces Hua onto his knees.

HUA Do you know what
what you are holding in your hands?

Do you know what you are burning,
little girl?

That is worth more
than your life.

Ling throws the costume into the bin.

LING   We have to march forward!—

HUA   Thousands of years from now,
when our country is nothing
but a distant memory,
all that truly remains
will be our paintings,
our poetry,
books,
our plays and operas,
songs and lullabys.

A wealthy legacy of our accomplishments.

But with your short-sighted
high-mindedness,
you destroy them
without a thought.

It's you.
That need to be held responsible.
That need to be hanged.
For the ruthless
and senseless murder
of our civilization!

Ling applauds.

LING   Bravo.
A wonderful performance.

Ling produces a photograph. Ling throws it to Hua.

LING   What do you have to say
        about this?

Hua picks up the photograph.

HUA   It's—
       a photograph—

LING   Of you.
        In a dress—

HUA   It was after a performance.
       I was in costume.
       The White-Haired Damsel—

LING   In a dress.

        Singing and dancing,
        like a trained monkey,
        in front of western imperialists.

        Have you no face?

HUA   I was representing China.
       It was a state-sanctioned tour.
       1935.
       I was in Russia
       and they were—

LING   Sergei Eisenstein.
        Bertolt Brecht.
        Important influential foreigners.

        And behind them,
        see?

        Russian politicians.

HUA   What are you implying?—

LING   Espionage.

       Passing state secrets
       to the Russians.

HUA   That is not true—

Ling takes the photograph from Hua and replaces it with the little red book. Ling returns to her chair and sits.

LING   Before I leave you,
       dear Comrade Hua,
       please turn to page six
       of our leader's little red book.

       I believe
       you will find his policy
       quite useful.

       "Lenient treatment
       for those who confess,
       and severe punishment
       for those who remain stubborn."

       Think carefully
       about which category
       you wish
       to belong.

Hua looks at the little red book. Ling looks at the photograph.

7.

Back stage.

Sonja stands at the edge of the deck.

From the previous scene, Ling walks to the metal bin with the photograph. Ling studies the photograph.

Ling notices Sonja.

LING So you are writing a book
about Comrade Hua.

SONJA Yes—

LING How many people
do you think
will read this book?

SONJA My last book sold
five million copies—

Ling walks towards Sonja.

LING Don't you want to interview me?

Holds out her hand.

I think I can provide—

Sonja doesn't take Ling's hand.

SONJA Not particularly.

LING I think I can supply the—

SONJA What part of "no," don't you understand?

Ling puts her hand down, walks away and secretly pockets the photograph.

LING Well,
you'll have a long wait
for Comrade Hua then.

Ling starts to tear and burn papers and books.

SONJA What have you done to Master Hua?

LING   We've placed *Comrade* Hua
in solitary confinement
for two weeks until he regains his senses
and confesses his—

LING and SONJA   Crimes against the people.

LING   Well,
so you know.

Ling eyes Sonja suspiciously. Sonja studies Ling curiously.

SONJA   I presume
you have some books to burn.

LING   I'll be watching you.

SONJA   And I,
you.

Ling exits.

8.

Back stage.

Hua and Sonja laughing.

SONJA   And you told the Red Guard,
under interrogation—

HUA   Yes—

SONJA   About the evils
of the Cultural Revolution.

You said—
wait, I remember—
you said

"It's you
that need to be hanged—"

SONJA and HUA   "For the ruthless
and senseless murder
of our civilization!"

SONJA   It was brilliant.
Absolutely brilliant.

HUA   I thought so too.

SONJA   You know,
I've always been interested
in your life, your work.

HUA   So the Americans have also heard of me.

SONJA   Well, no.

I scoured the libraries
the Internet,
nothing.

Dug into a slew of magazines
journals, books,
nothing.

Only a couple of brief mentions,
odd footnotes.
Here and there.
About you.
In the early days.

HUA   You Americans
have always been wanting in culture.

SONJA   But I remember
a story

about how you made Mao Zedong cry
in one of your performances.
What a wonderful anecdote
to tell your children.

HUA   It's so long ago.
A minor incident.

SONJA   How can you forget
such a moment?

HUA   I cannot remember the details.

Sonja puts the tape recorder in front of Hua.

HUA   It was the
Festival of the Hungry Ghosts.
The ninth month.
Many years ago—

SONJA   I thought
it was the Ching Ming Festival
in the—
I remember I—

HUA   It was the
Festival of the Hungry Ghosts

SONJA   No, no.
I'm sure of it—
Ching Ming—

HUA   Is this my moment?
Or yours?

Beat.

SONJA   Yours.

Beat.

Ling observes Sonja and Hua's interaction at a corner of the stage without being noticed.

HUA   Well then,
        it was the Festival of the Hungry Ghosts.
        The ninth month.
        Many years ago.

(Animatedly)

        A night like any other.
        I was putting on my makeup for the show.

        Then Stage Manager Kong
        frantically burst
        into my dressing room,
        shrieking
        "Chairman Mao is in the audience!"

        Chairman Mao in the audience.
        I couldn't care less
        if the Queen of Sheba
        was sitting in the front row.
        I was working!

        I decided not to fuss.
        After all,
        he was coming to see me.
        Not vice versa.

        I calmly applied my makeup.
        Prepared for the show.
        Concentrated on the performance.
        Sipped my hot tea.
        Like I always did.

(Childishly)

But,
at the last minute,
I simply couldn't resist
the aching temptation
to see this man who had taken
all of China by storm.

So,
when no one was looking
I quickly tiptoed
to the side wings,
scurried behind the painted scenery,
and desperately tried
to catch a glimpse of him.
I couldn't find him.
Where was he?

Where?

Where?

Where?

And
there he was.

In a sea of noisy farmers,
peasants, and workers.
Chairman Mao,
sitting there,
in my theater,
with his bodyguards.
eating steamed pork dumplings.

What a sight!

SONJA   Were you disappointed?

I was excited meeting Oprah Winfrey—

HUA   But I was in the presence of greatness!

Chairman Mao turned China around.
Unified a fractured nation.
Things were improving.

And this legend,
this god,
was in the audience,
watching my work,
watching me.

SONJA   And how did he react?

Ling enters and tells Sonja the story. Hua does not look at Ling. Two realities are happening in this scene.

LING   Chairman Mao
he broke into tears—

HUA   Bawling.
Like a baby.

I do have
that kind of effect
over people—

SONJA   A true moment.

The White Haired Damsel opera,
wasn't it?—

HUA   Yes—

LING   I was only twelve years old then.

I slipped away
from the house
and ran to the theater
in the center of town.

Once there,
I pierced through the rowdy crowds,
and found myself
an empty seat.

I sat there,
with sticky sesame candy
and hot tea in my hands,
watching the opera.
but I never ate.

I couldn't.

I just sat there.

Mesmerized.

Through his delicate song,
I was lifted.
Transported.

All I heard was this longing.
This terrible,
aching longing.
About how the White-Haired Damsel
missed her home.

Before I knew it,
I had tears.
Streaming,
streaking down my cheeks.

Hua begins to act out the opera.

HUA When we got to the part
where I was being raped
by the evil landlord,
Chairman Mao frantically shouted—

HUA and **LING**   "We've got to have the revolution!"—

LING   But the grand actor—

HUA   I continued singing—

LING   Seamlessly!

Ignoring the Chairman's ranting.
As if he didn't exist—

HUA   The bodyguards tried to calm Chairman Mao,
but he brushed them away.

Suddenly,
he struggled to his feet.
Shouting for help
in rescuing me!—

Hua and Ling laugh.

LING   As always,
his bodyguards had unbuckled his belt.
You see,
the Chairman had a big belly,
and that made it more comfortable for him
to sit through the performance—

HUA   And when he stood up—

LING   His pants
dropped to the floor!

HUA   But the Chairman.
He just stood.
Facing me.

Tears flowed from his wet eyes.
He was hardly conscious
of what was going on.

When the opera was finished,
he rushed to the stage
to congratulate me.

(Reaches out with his hand as if to shake hands)

Holding his pants with one hand.
And the other.
Fiercely clutching my hand.
Shaking it.

SONJA   Did Chairman Mao say anything to you?

Hua looks at his hand.

HUA   Yes.
He said—
we were
his messengers.
We were
the party's foot soldiers.
And that
he was proud of us.

LING   Then Chairman Mao smiled.
And disappeared into
the shouting cheering crowds.

HUA   That was a moment.
My moment—

LING   A moment I'll never forget.

Beat.

SONJA   Then in 1966—

HUA   That's enough for today—

SONJA In 1966—

LING The Cultural Revolution—

HUA That's enough—

LING The Chairman,
at the bidding of his wife,
Jiang Qing,
had all of China's art
literature music plays operas
destroyed—

HUA I said
that's enough for today—

LING The cultural legacy
of thousands and thousands of years.
Torn into pieces.
Thrown into flames.

SONJA And what happened then?

HUA I never sang again.

9.

On stage.

Ling stands on a chair. She dances and sings the White-Haired
Damsel *aria. Holding his training stick, Hua listens with his head
hung low and his eyes closed.*

Both Hua and Ling are exhausted and testy.

HUA Sing—

LING Again?—

HUA Again—

LING I can't—

HUA Again,
Ling—

LING Please—

HUA You can.
Again—

LING I'm tired.

Beat.

HUA Where are you?—

LING In the mountains—

HUA Ah yes,
the mountains.

Can you smell
the crisp mountain air?
Feel
the cool shadow of trees?
Can you hear
the gentle rustling of leaves
as the wind rushes
between the branches?

LING No.

Hua lifts his arms up, demonstrating hand movements.

HUA Ling,
lift your hands up.

Gently.

Like this.

Again.

Ling lifts her arms up, imitating Hua's movements.

LING   My arms.
        They feel heavy—

HUA   And remember,
        who are you?—

LING   The White-Haired Damsel—

HUA   A servant girl—

LING   A servant girl—

HUA   You were brutally raped
        by the evil landlord—

LING   Raped by the evil landlord—

HUA   You fled
        to the faraway mountains—

LING   Faraway mountains—

HUA   And you just bore
        his illegitimate child—

LING   I know just how she feels.

HUA   Again.

        From the top.

LING   Can we take a rest?

HUA   We will take a rest
        once you get it right.

Hua slams his stick onto the flow. Ling sings and dances.

HUA   No.
Not like that.

Hua adjusts her arm and leg movements with his stick.

HUA   You have bad posture.
It's not ladylike.

LING   You would know.

HUA   Yes, I would.

Everything you see
in my work
is earned.
Not given.
The point is
your femininity
must be earned.

LING   I think I would know what femininity is.

HUA   Then you have much more to learn.

Hua slams his stick onto the floor. Ling gets down on the chair and dances around the stage. Hua sits. He looks at Ling's dancing.

Look!
Look at you!
You walk like a duck!

Why do you think
men have undertaken
and mastered women's parts
in Chinese theater
for generations?

HUA   It's because—

Ling rolls her eyes and mocks Hua while she dances.

HUA AND LING   We know
                how women are to behave.
                How they are to move.
                To talk.
                To grace the earth.

                Femininity is created for men and by men.
                Femininity is an art.

HUA   Now
       you have the opportunity to claim
       what is rightfully yours
       on stage,
       you shirk.
       Bellyache.
       Complain.
       Again.
       Lift your hands.

       Gently.

       Lithely.

Ling stops what she's doing and sits on the floor in exhausted defiance.

LING   I can't anymore.

Hua turns away from her, and leaves.

HUA   Then give up!
       Throw it all away!

       And I thought you wanted to be an actor.
       An artist.

45

LING I do,
but—

Hua abruptly exits. Ling slowly gets up from the floor.

Ling looks at the departing Hua.

Beat.

LING From the top?

Hua stops in his tracks.

HUA From the top.

And put some heart into it.

Sing!

LING Yes.

HUA Sing.

Louder.

Clearer.

Sing.

To the gods.

Ling dances and sings an aria.

Hua closes his eyes and listens.

10.

On stage.

Ling is standing center stage. She is holding a wooden pole.

Sonja is frozen in fear.

LING   Bring out the feudalist pig!

Suddenly, stagehands on all sides of the stage start to rumble their chairs, creating a frightening cacophony.

A stagehand with his head wrapped in a gunny sack is hauled onstage by another stagehand.

Ling looks him apprehensively. Then she pushes him onto the floor. The stagehand lies in a pool of light.

LING   Confess!

Confess!

Confess!

Confess!

Ling kicks the stagehand. The more she kicks, the harder her kick becomes. Every time Ling kicks the stagehand, the other stagehands rumbling the chairs slam their chairs on the floor to suggest the violent kicks.

LING   Confess!

Confess!

Confess!

Confess!

Ling stops. She looks up at the balcony and nods. Ling grabs a pole and raises it to strike the stagehand.

LING   Confess!

11.

Back stage.

Sonja is smoking.

From the previous scene, an exhausted Ling enters with a wooden pole.

Mischievously, Ling slams her pole on the desk, making Sonja jump.

SONJA There you are.

    So you were once Master Hua's student—

LING I thought
   you didn't want to interview me
   You said—

SONJA I need to speak with you.
    Your point of view—

LING No—

SONJA It would be important,
    invaluable
    if I am writing the book—

LING What part of "no,"
   don't you understand, Sonja?

SONJA From what my two eyes have witnessed,
    Comrade Ling,
    you are not going to be
    quite a pretty picture in my book.

LING What do you mean?
   I did all the right—

SONJA The cruel interrogations,
    the burning of books,
    the beating of political prisoners,
    the dreadful dancing—

    Shall I go on?

Don't you want to clear the air?
Set the record straight?

Silence.

SONJA   Have a seat.

Ling sits down.

SONJA   Cigarette?

Ling is obviously uncomfortable with the cigarette smoke.

LING   Will you be smoking
throughout this—?

SONJA   Yes.

It's a bad habit.
But I say,
why fight it?

Especially when it's larger than you are.
It's better to yield,
to succumb.

(*Takes out her tape recorder*)

Isn't that why you became a revolutionary?

LING   I thought
we were here to talk about
my apprenticeship
with Master Hua.

SONJA   You know,
come to think of it,
you resemble the heroine
in my last novel.

You are exactly how I pictured her:
Simple.
Not too bright.
Heart of steel.
Cute bangs.
Sensible.
Whiny voice.
Bit on the grumpy side.
Dies at the end of the story.

Come to think of it,
all of my female characters
look like you.

LING (*Sarcastically*) Really?

SONJA Have you read it?
It's called *Bound Feet, Bound Lives?*

LING Vivid title—

SONJA My protagonist:
About your age.
A plain Chinese village girl.
Bound feet.
Bound
to a loveless arranged marriage
to a ruthless Communist cadre leader,
old enough
to be her grandfather.
Relationship's not meant to be.
In the end,
as always,
suicide for her.

LING Tragic.

SONJA   But not a downer.
         It's got real funny moments.
         Uplifting in parts.
         You should check it out.
         It's a must read.

LING   Arranged marriages and bound feet
         are a thing of the past.
         What you just described
         are counterrevolutionary ideas—

Sonja blows cigarette smoke in Ling's face. Ling storms off.

SONJA   So,
         you were once Master Hua's student.

Ling stops.

LING   Yes.

SONJA   Why did you want to be in Beijing opera?

Beat.

LING   Well,
         I've always wanted to be an actor,
         an opera star—

SONJA   Really?
         I couldn't tell.

LING   Ever since I saw the master on stage.

         From young,
         I knew that it was fruitless.
         Women were not allowed to be in the opera.
         Parts were assigned to boys and men.
         Even roles that called specifically for women.

But one day,
I plucked up my courage
and persuaded him,
one of the greatest Beijing opera stars,
to let me study under him.

Hua enters, not looking at Ling but at his script.

Ling runs around Hua while speaking to Sonja.

HUA   No women are allowed in the profession.
Go away.

LING   I would walk with him
as he made his way to the theater
every evening.

HUA   Why do you want to do this?
You should get married.
Go home.

LING   Then
I'd wait for his show to finish
and walk him back home.

Asking,
asking him.
Again
and again.

HUA   Try embroidery.
I know just the person who can teach you.
How about calligraphy?

LING   Hounded him daily.
On the streets.

HUA   Pottery?

LING At home.

HUA Poetry?

LING At the theater.

HUA Cooking?

LING In the teahouse.
I was relentless.

HUA You are relentless!
If you like the theater so much,
have a taste of it.

Hua dances.

LING I was so happy!

Every day
I arrived at the theater early.

Cleaned his makeup table.
Hand washed his costumes.
Lit his cigarettes.
Brewed his favorite tea.

Watched him from the wings
as he leapt into the air,
fought with demons and spirits,
romanced famous generals
and rural peasants
with song and dance.
Watched him die.
Again and again.

It was heaven.

HUA If you want to learn,
just shut up and watch me.

Watch me.

Closely.

LING He was so beautiful.
He made me forget.
Where I am.
Who I am.

HUA Are you watching?

To Hua.

LING Yes.
Yes.

HUA Good.

To Sonja.

LING But
I wanted to do more than watch.

I wanted to get up on stage.
Feel the caress of creaky floorboards
with my dancing feet.
Feel the heat of lights on my face,
my body.

I wanted to sing,
loud and strong,
thundering through the theater.

Hear the cascading shouts,
applause
as I take my bows
on stage.
People calling my name,
throwing flowers

So
I kept begging him,
tried all kinds of ruses
to get him
to say "yes."

(*To Hua*)

You were so magnificent
when you sang to the Imperial Court
about injustice.

I was so moved.
See.

(*Points to her cheeks*)

Tears.
Tears—

HUA (*Grunts*) Hmm!

LING You know I'm ready!
I've done this stupid apprenticeship
for more than a year!
I'm sick of it!
I'm not your little servant girl,
Picking up after your royal highness!
You're just too pigheaded to see I'm ready!—

HUA Hmm!

LING I love the theater.
I can't wait to get here every day.
Watching you work.
Learning from you.
I'm so lucky just to be here.
I just love—

HUA   Hmm!

LING   I tried everything.
Flattery.
Anger.
Passion.
Reason.
But the stubborn old fool wouldn't listen.

HUA   All right, all right!
Stop your whining and conniving little tricks.

Come here,
every day,
four hours before the show.

I'll train you.

LING   And we trained,
for four years,
on a bare stage,
and no one in the company knew.

He was my mentor.

When I saw him on stage,
I knew I wanted to be
just like him.

SONJA   And did you?
Become like him?

LING   Yes.

(*Beat*)

And better.

12

Back stage.

SONJA So you took on a female protégé—
A teenager—

HUA Yes—
I remember when I was in New York—

SONJA Her name was Ling.

    . This was in 1962.
    Despite the strict traditions
    imposed by your Chinese opera troupe—

HUA Yes—yes—
New York—Broadway—
I saw a play—

SONJA You defied strict traditions.
You started training women
to take on roles—

HUA Enough—

SONJA I have only a few more questions.
In 1962—

HUA I said enough—

SONJA Just one more then.
In 1962 you—

HUA That's enough for today, Sonja.
I'm actually tired of hearing myself
talk for once.

Pause.

SONJA   Then I should go.
        Let you get some—

HUA   Stay.

(*Gestures for Sonja to sit*)

        Please.

(*Beat*)

        Tell me about yourself, Sonja.

SONJA   What do you want to know?

HUA   Everything.
      Anything.

SONJA   I'm afraid there's not much to tell.

HUA   Everyone has a story.

SONJA   I really don't have one.

HUA   You come
      from a country of reinvention,
      you are an author
      and you can't come up—

SONJA   Why are you prying—

HUA   I would like
      to get to know you better, Sonja.

SONJA   My books—

HUA   Beyond your books, Sonja,
      who is this woman before me?

SONJA   I work a lot.
        Travel and—
        It's been a very busy few years—

        You know,
        I'm not sure.

HUA   Perhaps that's why you write.

SONJA   Perhaps.

HUA   What about your family?
        Are they—?

SONJA   I have—none.

HUA   Friends?

SONJA   A few here and there.

HUA   You must be very lonely.

SONJA   I don't have time
        to be lonely.

HUA   Any hobbies?
        Interests?

SONJA   Well,
        I have dabbled in Chinese opera.

HUA   You and Chinese opera?

        Tell me.

SONJA   When I was young—

HUA   Many, many years ago—

SONJA   Yes—
        Many, many years ago.

        I left Hong Kong for America—

HUA   But I thought you were American—

SONJA   I am, now.

I entered the country illegally.
On an oil tanker.

Through some connections,
I worked as a waitress.

Can you believe it?
Me.
A waitress.

HUA   Yes, I can.

SONJA   On my free evenings,
rare and few,
I got to do some acting
in Chinese street theater.

HUA   I think that's wonderful.
You in the theater.

SONJA   But I soon left.

HUA   Why?

SONJA   I found Chinese opera
to be a dying art in America.

Worse still,
the audiences were paltry.
Mainly,
they were the silver-haired old folks
who came in small but dedicated droves.

The young ones didn't come.
Instead they stayed home,
watched TV,
went to the movies.
They said

the operas didn't mean anything to them.
Their lives were reflected
more clearly in sitcoms.

I didn't see the point.
Performing night after night.
To a small handful of audiences.

It wasn't worth it.

HUA "Wasn't worth it?"

There's a reason
why Chinese opera has endured for centuries!

It's an art.
An elevated art—

SONJA I know,
but no one came—

HUA Stories and histories.
It speaks to the hearts of people—

SONJA No one came—

HUA And everyone in the theater—

SONJA No one came—

HUA Dedicates their lives to the opera.
How can it die?
How can anyone not come—?

SONJA No one came.
No one.

Silence.

SONJA After a while,
the old audiences died off

and there weren't enough audiences
to warrant the opera's existence.

The city council stopped funding it.
The benevolent societies
didn't have enough money.

Later,
all the costumes, props, and sets
were stored away
in nondescript warehouses
in the Bowery.

Dust,
dirt soon carpeted the silks and sequins.

And
Chinese street opera became extinct.

HUA   Chinese opera.
Extinct.

I can't believe it.

SONJA   I know.

Silence.

HUA   I've been—
I'm sorry—

Please tell me more about yourself.

SONJA   Then
came the grand detour.
With nothing to do in the evenings,
I enrolled in a few English classes
at the local community college.

There,

my English as a Second Language instructor,
forty-something Bob Pickford
assigned us
to write short stories—

HUA   Pickford.

SONJA   My first ex-husband.

HUA   First?

SONJA   Yes—
of many—

HUA   I don't think we have the time.

SONJA   Bob was most intrigued,
most fascinated,
by my experiences,
my perceptions of Asia.

He often encouraged me,
persuaded me to write
about my time there.

At first
I didn't know where to start.

I stared
at a blank piece of paper
for the longest time.

Then,
as if by magic,
my yellow Bic pen inked the first word.

Words bled into sentences,
sentences melded into paragraphs,
paragraphs into a story.
Stories about—

HUA   Home.

SONJA   Yes.

When I turned them in,
Bob simply went crazy over them.

He sent them
around to magazines,
newspapers,
short story contests,
publishing houses.

The stories eventually got published.
Got serious attention.

The next thing I know,
Random House approached me
and they were published
in a book.

HUA   Then success!

SONJA   Then divorce.

HUA   You became rich and famous—

SONJA   Sold millions of copies.
Six months
on the *New York Times* Best-Sellers List—

HUA   We should learn from you.
Be commercial—

SONJA   *The Oprah Winfrey Show,*
Talk show circuits,
the *People* magazine cover story—

HUA   Opening night galas,
parties,
paparazzi—

SONJA Yes—

HUA Yes—

SONJA They were the best days of my life.

Beat.

HUA I remember all that, too.

Beat.

So you made it.

SONJA I did well.
Very well.

HUA Then
you are an artist.

SONJA Am I?

HUA Aren't you?
In China,
after a lifetime of ridicule and
disrespect, you know you've made it
when they throw you a banquet
serving roast pig
when you're dead.

Hua and Sonja laugh.

Hua starts to dance.

HUA Come
join me.

SONJA I can't presume to—

HUA Come.

Sonja joins Hua and they dance together beautifully.

HUA   So
you know this dance.

SONJA   I guess.

HUA   You see,
your years in Chinese opera,
they are not at all wasted.

Sonja and Hua continue dancing.

13.

Back stage.

Ling is singing the White-Haired Damsel *aria offstage.*

Hua is peeking through the curtain, nodding and smiling in approval of Ling's performance.

Sound of thunderous applause.

Hua quickly runs away from the curtain and looks at the floor.

In costume, Ling walks in wearing Hua's White-Haired Damsel costume that we've seen in earlier scenes.

LING   Are you feeling much better?

HUA   Look.
The floor.
It's dirty—

LING   Your diarrhea—

HUA   All gone.
All gone.

LING   Really.
        So fast?

HUA   The miracle of Eastern medicine.

LING   I don't believe you.

HUA   Is it my stomach or yours?

LING   I see.

HUA   "I see. I see."
        If you see so much,
        why is the floor still so filthy?

Ling changes out of her costume.

HUA   Where are my cigarettes?

LING   There.
        In your dressing table drawer.
        Top left.

HUA   One night I'm not here,
        and you've completely taken to
        rearranging my dressing table.

        You must be anxious to have me
        in a permanent state of diarrhea.

LING   You should stop smoking so much.

HUA   I smoke what I want,
        when I want.

LING   You must be feeling much better.

HUA   Of course I'm better.
        Leave me alone.

LING You should have gone on then.

HUA Yes.
Maybe I should have.

Silence.

LING So—
did you see?

HUA See what?

LING What I did.

HUA Out there?

LING On stage.

Yes.

Beat.

HUA You walk like a man.
Speak like a man.
Sing like a man.
What's wrong with you?

LING Ah.

HUA Don't "ah" me.
Everything I taught you.
All in the toilet.

What did I tell you?
Time and time again?
It's got to be what?

LING Big.

HUA Yes.
It's got to be big, big, big.

Did I see "big?"
No, I didn't see "big."
What's wrong with you?

Beat.

LING Did you know the audiences thought
I was you
out there?

HUA Not in a million years.

LING They kept calling me.
By your name.

HUA They are blind.

LING They kept applauding.
Cheering.
I must have done something right.

HUA You mustn't let the audiences
determine the quality of your work.

Sometimes
I don't think
they even know what they are watching.

Beat.

LING (*Smiling*) So you liked it?

HUA Liked what?

LING Stop teasing me.

Did you like it,
what I did?

HUA No—

LING   You liked it—

HUA   I said no—

LING   You liked it—

HUA   You'll never be good enough.

Where's my tea?

14.

Back stage.

From the previous scene, Ling rehearses her dance on stage.

HUA   (*Yelling to Ling*)   Don't think
I cannot see you!
Faster faster faster!
What's the matter with you?

SONJA   Aren't you a little too hard on her?

HUA   She's not good enough.

(*To Ling*)

Again!

SONJA   I think she's pretty good.
And she tries very hard.

Look.

Isn't that beautiful?

Hua studies Ling for a moment.

HUA   No.

Hua looks away and packs his things.

70

SONJA You're leaving?

HUA It's late.

SONJA What about Ling?

HUA Ling will be absolutely fine.
She's done this before.

SONJA Aren't you going to accompany her home?
It's nearly midnight.

HUA She can sleep back stage
if it gets too late.
There's a cot here.

Besides,
she has much to learn,
much to rehearse.

SONJA She must get lonely.

HUA She'll survive.
It'll toughen her up.

SONJA Where are you going?

HUA Why are you full of questions tonight?

SONJA Are you going home?

HUA No.
To Stage Manager Kong's house.

SONJA Why do you spend so much time
with Stage Manager Kong?

You work with him.
Drink and eat.
Play mah-jonng and cards with him.

HUA Because he's my friend.

SONJA Didn't you have a wife?

HUA Yes,
I married her
to save her
from a life of poverty.

We were happy
until she died of—

You see, Sonja,
we all have our stories.

And like you,
there are some stories
we rather not hear
not revisit again,
for fear of pain,
for fear of regret.

SONJA I see.

HUA Good night, Sonja.

(*Shouts to Ling*)

I can't hear you from here!

Sing!
Sing!

Hua exits as both Ling and Sonja look at him, the former with sadness, the latter with anger.

15

Back stage.

Ling is rehearsing a dance, while Hua is rehearsing the same dance on stage.

SONJA   What are you doing?

LING   Rehearsing.

SONJA   Again?

LING   Have to be good enough.

Beat.

SONJA   He's always bossing you around.
Why don't you tell him off?

LING   Would you?

SONJA   Not in a million years.

Both Sonja and Ling laugh.

Pause.

LING   I've been meaning to ask—

SONJA   Yes?

LING   Since you are a successful and famous author—
artist to artist—
do you have any advice for me?

SONJA   Surely, Master Hua—

LING   He's not forthcoming with his—
all I get from him are growls and criticisms.

I've been thinking about—writing.

SONJA   Writing?

LING Yes.
I have some ideas for a play.

SONJA What about acting?

LING There must be more to Chinese opera
than stodgy legends and fairy tales—

SONJA I see.

Beat.

LING So what inspires you?

SONJA A lot of things.

LING What do you write about?

SONJA The Asian experience.
About who we are,
and how far we've come.

LING You mentioned *Bound Feet, Bound Lives*—

SONJA Yes.

LING What kind of book—

SONJA Romance.

LING You write to entertain, then?

SONJA Yes,
but my novels are much more than that.

They are thinly disguised.
Crack the surface,
you will find my novels are also
about the Asian—

LING   Are all your books about that?
        That one genre?
        Romance.

SONJA   Yes,
            but all my stories are different.

            I change the location,
            the time period.
            It's another variation on a theme.

            And it's another book.
            Another best-seller.
            Another movie-of-the-week—

LING   You do your art for money then—

SONJA   Listen,
            you asked for advice.

            I'm just telling you
            the way it is.

            I give my readers
            a people, a culture,
            a language, a country
            they've vaguely heard of,
            but will never experience firsthand.

            Deposit them somewhere exotic,
            say Bangkok, Hong Kong, Singapore.
            And I'm their trusted tour guide,
            holding their hands,
            venturing deep
            into the heartland of the Orient.

            After they spend thirty dollars
            and a couple of weeks
            buried in my words,

they will have understood us a little better.
Understood how we suffered,
how we lived,
how we loved, ·
and how we cried.

LING So your readers believe what you write?

SONJA The funny thing is
I can give them Iowa
and they won't know the difference.

You see,
I'm credible.

Look at my face.
My readers see I'm Asian.
One hundred percent.
The real McCoy.

If I say this is white,
it's white.
If I say this is black,
it's black.

And if I say
this is one hundred percent pure Chinese,
it is.

LING How can you not want them
to see us for who we are?

As artists, it's our responsibility—

SONJA It's not a question
of how *we* want them to see us.
It's how *they* want to see us.

(*Beat*)

After my first book was published,
I was thrust into
an unexpected fire of success and accolades.

When it came time to write the second,
I decided to shine a harsh light
on the real faces of immigrant Asian America.
My life
in the red white and blue.

I filled my stories
with the daily plights,
triumphs, and hopes
of these shadow people.

It was my proudest work.

LING   That's wonderful.

SONJA   But,
no one flocked to buy the book.

Instead,
copies of *Shadow People*
were found abandoned,
remaindered
in a cemetery of unread books.

It was then I understood:
the buying public doesn't want
to see us as flesh and blood.

They want to see us
bathed in glorious,
misty hues of magic and smoke.

They want stories of Fu Manchu,
barbaric gods

with twelve arms wielding sabers,
polygamist men
with their entourage of Chinese wives,
geisha girls, acrobats, Beijing opera—

LING   You are exactly like
Master Hua and his fluffy operas!

SONJA   What do you mean—?

LING   You give them what they want—

SONJA   Yes,
and why not?

Do you think it's only the white folks
who eat up what I have to say?
A large number of my readers are Asians.
Asians who have no idea
what their own histories are.
These Asian Americans are
never Asian enough,
never American enough.

Straddling two worlds
that have no place for them.
They hunger for a sense of home.

They crave my books.
And I never let them down.
I give them a sense of belonging.
I give them history.

LING   You ply them with lies!
You invent their histories!

SONJA   If you want authenticity,
there are always family stories and secrets

told over the dinner table.
Bizarre Oriental customs
from a hazy childhood—

LING   Why are you so proud of this?—
You have a responsibility—

SONJA   I have no responsibility.
Except to myself and to my craft.
I love what I do.
No apologies—

LING   Everything you write,
says something about you
and about the world you see.
Everything you don't,
does the same.
Everything has consequences—

SONJA   What consequences?
I'm simply exercising
my freedom of expression.
Freedom of speech—

LING   There's no freedom in art.
Don't you realize
how dangerous
your art
can be to your readers?
You have the power to change lives,
change minds—

SONJA   And what is more dangerous?
Listening to the artist
or the government—?

LING All art is political—

SONJA Is that why the Red Guards
    want to control art?
    With their Cultural Revolution?
    Because they are afraid
    of the opposing point of view—

LING Because
    they recognize the power of art.
    But
    in the wrong hands—

SONJA The artists' hands—

LING What you create—

SONJA Beauty—

LING Decadence—

SONJA Humanity—

LING Filth—

SONJA Truth—

LING Lies—

SONJA Hope—

LING *We* want art to have responsibilities—

SONJA Who's we?—

LING The people—

SONJA The Red Guards?

(*Beat*)

    You?

Silence.

LING You are a fraud.

SONJA The lesson of people living in glass houses.

LING I will never end up like you.

Ling storms out.

16.

On stage.

An exhausted Hua stands on a chair, wearing a tall white dunce cap and a placard with Chinese characters around his neck.

Ling paces in the front of the house.

LING (*Shouting*) Again!

HUA (*Shouting*) Without the People's Army,
the people will have nothing!

LING Again!

HUA Without the People's Army,
the people will have nothing!

LING Again!

HUA Without the People's Army,
the people will have nothing!

Pause.

Ling looks out into the balcony.

LING He's gone.

HUA Are you sure?

LING Yes. I don't see him in the theater.

HUA Where?

Ling indicating with her eyes.

LING Up there.
In the balcony.

There.

He usually sits
by the aisle
in the back row.

HUA I see.

LING How are you?

HUA I'm fine.

LING What do you need?

HUA I need to sit.
Sit down.

LING I don't think you should.
Just in case,
he comes back.

HUA You are right.

LING Water?

HUA Please.

Ling runs on stage and gives Hua a cup of water.

LING Here.
Drink it quickly.

Hua drinks quickly. Ling takes the cup away from him.

HUA How have you been, Ling?

LING I'm sorry.

HUA It's all right.

LING I wish I could undo everything.
I would.

HUA I know.

LING You know I would never have done it.
I just didn't know.
I didn't.

HUA Shh.

Beat.

I've been meaning to ask for many weeks.
Is it true?

LING What are you talking about?

HUA Stage Manager Kong.
About what happened to him.

Beat.

LING It's true.

Hua getting emotional.

HUA I thought it was—
A lie—
To make me—
To break me—
I thought—it was a lie.

LING   They made me—
        they said I had to prove I was one of them—
        that I was worthy of being a Red Guard—
        of being the chairman's soldier.

Ling walks away from Hua and walks to the downstage area where she kicked and beat the stagehand in scene 10. The same pool of light appears. Ling looks at it and kneels speaking to it.

LING   They brought Stage Manager Kong here
        to the theater one night—
        put him on stage—
        put him in a circle where he—
        there were eight of us—

HUA   I don't want to hear—

LING   Put a filthy gunnysack over his head—
        Pushed him around—
        we had sticks—
        we beat him—

HUA   Stop—

LING   Some others kicked him—
        kicked him around like he was a football—
        they made us call him names—

HUA   Stop—

LING   I kicked him!—
        kicked him!—
        Stage Manager Kong—
        he didn't even scream—
        didn't make a single noise—
        then he stopped moving—
        when I finally took the gunnysack off him—

84

HUA Stop—

LING I saw his bloody face—

HUA Stop!—

LING Couldn't recognize him—

HUA Stop!—

LING His face was swollen—
red—
with welts and cuts—

HUA (*Interrupting*)   Stop!
Please.

Ling slams her fists on the ground.

Silence.

LING I can't do this anymore.
I can't—

HUA You have to—

LING I can't stand it any longer—

Hua gets down from the chair and rushes over to Ling.

HUA You must save yourself—

LING Please—
don't make me—

Hua tries to get Ling to stand up.

HUA You are my daughter,
are you not?

Beat.

Aren't you?

Beat.

LING Yes.

HUA Then behave like one.

Hua gets up and stands on the chair.

HUA Obey me.
Remember what I taught you.

LING *Ren.*

HUA Yes.
Ren.

You must.
For all our sakes.

LING *Ren.*

Beat.

HUA Are you eating properly?

LING Yes.

HUA You look so thin.

Ling looks up into the house.

LING Papa, he's back.

Beat.

LING Again!

HUA. (*Shouting*) Without the People's Army,
the people will have nothing!

LING   Again!

HUA   Without the People's Army,
the people will have nothing!

LING   Again!

HUA   Without the People's Army,
the people will have nothing!

17.

Back stage.

Hua putting on his makeup. Ling sits on the floor.

LING   Sing it to me again, Papa.

HUA   Later.
Let me finish putting on my makeup.

LING   Papa, please.

HUA   Papa has to play the White-Haired Damsel tonight.

LING   Mama used to sing it to me.

Pause.

HUA   Mama is not here anymore.

LING   I know.
She's dead.

HUA   Yes.

Aren't you tired of hearing it?

LING   Never.
Not if you sing it.

HUA How old are you, Ling?

LING Ten.

HUA Ten years old!
Aren't you old enough to sing by yourself?

LING But I want you to sing it, Papa.

HUA I have to get ready for the show—

LING Please?

Hua sings it quickly.

HUA "Gently, gently
She dances to her father's voice
Gently, gently
In *mei hua* blossom night"

Hua looks at Ling. He stops applying his makeup.

HUA Come,
sing with me.

HUA and **LING** "Gently, gently
Mei hua fades to winter white
Little girl child
She's no longer in sight

Gently, gently
Mei hua flower blossoms sway
Gently, gently
Her father misses her face"

Hua resumes putting on his makeup.

LING I love you, Papa.

On stage.

LING   He's back.

I see him.

I don't know if I can—

HUA   Yes.

You can.

You're an actress.

Let the scene begin.

Hua holds up a piece of paper.

LING   What is this?

HUA   My confession.

LING   You have not confessed your crimes.
These pages are blank.

HUA   I've nothing to confess.
I've done nothing wrong.

LING   We have proof of your crimes against the people.

HUA   Show me then.
This proof.

LING   We have the photograph.

HUA   You know
the photograph was insufficient evidence.

LING   We will show you leniency if you confess.

HUA   I'm not guilty!

LING   You are guilty
of corrupting the people with your art.

A grown man dressed like a woman!
Singing like a woman!

HUA   Illusion!—

LING   We also have proof
of your perverted licentious relationship
with your subordinate Stage Manager Kong—

HUA   There was nothing filthy about my relationship—

LING   Perverts lusting after each other—

HUA   We were friends!
Good friends!

LING (*Whispering*)   Papa,
just write something down.
Anything.

Lie.
Embellish.
Anything.

HUA (*Whispering*)   No.
I have done nothing wrong.

LING (*Out*)   Arrogant old fool!
You think
you can fool the people with your lies!

HUA   I will be vindicated by your investigations!

LING   Make it easy on yourself and confess!

HUA   No!

LING (*Whispering*)   Please, Papa!
Stop acting!

Write something down.
Anything.

Otherwise,
there will be severe consequences.

HUA (*Whispering*)   No.

LING (*Whispering*)   Papa,
this is serious!

HUA (*Whispering*)   So am I!

LING (*Whispering*)   Papa,
please!

Hua deliberately looks away from Ling and stares straight into the theater balcony.

HUA (*Out*)   I will be vindicated!
I have done nothing wrong!
Nothing!

Ling looks at Hua with a pained expression.

Ling exits and reenters with a gunnysack.

SONJA   No.

HUA   What is this, Ling?

The stagehands rumble their chairs on the floor creating a frightening cacophony.

LING   Shut up and put this over your head.

SONJA   Wait—
Stop—

HUA It's a gunnysack.

LING Put this over your head!

HUA I have done nothing wrong!

SONJA Stop!

Hua looks at Ling for a moment. Ling looks away.

LING We will—
kick some sense into you.
Make you reconsider your actions.
You will confess.

SONJA Ling!
You must stop this!
This cannot go—!

Hua turns to the theater balcony again.

HUA I have done nothing wrong.

Nothing.

Hua puts sack over his head and holds his head up high.

LING You will confess.

You will confess.

You will confess.

Ling hauls Hua to the same place where the stagehand in scene 10 was beaten. The same pool of light appears.

Sonja stands helplessly watching the two of them.

SONJA Ling, stop this!

Don't do it!

Don't!

LING   Confess!

Confess!

Confess!

Confess!

Ling lifts her pole into the air and just before it comes down onto Hua, all the stagehands slam their chairs on the floor in unison.

SONJA   No!

When everyone leaves the stage, the pool of light appears.

19.

Back stage.

Sonja was standing where we found her in the last scene.

Sonja walks to pick up the crumpled piece of paper. She then walks to the pool of light and touches it. Sonja shakes her head.

SONJA   Have to find another story—
this one is not—
it's too—

Maybe I can write about something else.

I know.

I'll pitch *White-Haired Damsel*
to the publisher instead.
Adapt it.
Finesse it into
something contemporary.
Something that could also be made
into a TV movie.

Sonja speaks into her tape recorder.

SONJA   *White-Haired Damsel.*

White-Haired Damsel.

Ling enters dressed as the Communist Party—sanctioned White-Haired Damsel. She enacts the following monologue to the Communist opera music.

Sonja pitches the following story in a Hollywood style.

SONJA   Okay.

The protagonist is a village girl.
Simple.
Cute bangs.
Sensible.
You get the picture.

She's got this father who committed suicide
because he cannot pay his rent.
Hence,
the relevance of rent control today.

Before he meets his maker or makers,
plural,
depending which Chinese religion
he kowtows to,
he sells the protagonist into slavery
to a landlord.

Slavery.
Black
and guilty liberal white
target audience potential here.

The girl is then brutally raped
by the landlord.
Think Jodie Foster in *The Accused*.

When he is away,
maybe he's out shopping for more slaves,
maidens, and what not,
our protagonist quickly escapes
into the wild mountains.
Very *Sound of Music*.

She then bears his child.
A tough broad.
Since she has no health care,
child care,
or cable,
she feeds on roots, rocks, and locusts,
whatever people living in mountains eat.

Her suffering and bad diet
make her hair turn ghostly white.
Clairol and Slim-Fast ad dollars here.

Our protagonist has no choice
but to live on the offerings
given to her by the villagers
who believe her a goddess.

Our story climaxes
with White-Haired Damsel
firing accusations against the landlord.

There's a legal trial to avenge her.
The village rejoices
that "age-old feudal bonds today
are cut away!"

Kinda like
the "Ding, dong, the witch is dead" sequence
with the Munchkins.

Music
music
music.

End of story.

(*Pause*)

Now,
that will be a tough sell,
even for TV.

Ling finishes her dance. She looks at Sonja.

LING   So there you are.

Beat.

SONJA   Yes,
here I am.

20.

Back stage.

From the last scene, Sonja follows Ling to the dressing room.

Ling takes off her revolutionary opera makeup.

LING   Our revolutionary opera
is an ugly mirror
that is held straight up
to your face
to reflect the needs and passions
of the people.

We must educate.
Challenge.
Enlighten.

And if we don't,
opera must be and should be obsolete—

SONJA Blah blah blah—

LING Are you taping all of this, Sonja?

SONJA So
you took over the theater.

Must be nice for you.

Ling grabs the tape recorder from Sonja and speaks into it.

LING (*Proudly*) I was the natural successor!

By an official directive,
I was made the new director
of the opera theater. I
am in charge of performances,
writing revolutionary plays,
training actors, and all matters
pertaining to this theater.

Is this tape recorder working?

SONJA (*Sarcastically*) Congratulations.

LING I knew
you'd be impressed.

SONJA (*Surprised*) And why's that?

LING I've been studying you.

SONJA Me?
Really.

LING   The way you walk and talk.
        The way you dress.
        Everything about you exudes
        confidence and success.

        You are a prime model of what women should
        be, even though I'm not convinced
        by your capitalist philosophies.

        Where you come from
        must encourage and empower you
        to be a woman.
        To be an equal.

SONJA   Ling,
        there is no such thing as true equality.

        Trust me.
        Even where I come from.

LING   Where I come from,
        males are unreasonably prized.

        If you are born female,
        you'll have the misfortune
        of being drowned in a river.
        Abandoned in some back wood.

        No one wants daughters
        because you inevitably lose them.

        They prefer sons.

SONJA   Does Master Hua feel the same way?
        Toward you?

LING   I think he would have
        preferred to have a son.

Heir to his theater,
his art.

SONJA   What did Mao say?
"Women hold up half the sky—"

LING   Yes!

SONJA   And what did Confucius say?
"Men are different from women—"

LING   "As the sky is different from the earth."

What bullshit!

Before I joined the Red Guards,
I was relegated to
the monotony of household chores.
Banned from schools,
literature, and higher learning.

Whatever you do,
You'll never be good enough.
You are judged for what you are,
and not who you are.

SONJA   But you are good.
From what I see of your work.

LING   Thank you.
You don't have to say—

Pause.

Sonja reaches and holds Ling's hand.

SONJA   I want to.
I mean it.

Beat.

LING You know,
   sometimes I say that to myself.
   Tell myself I'm good.
   Isn't it stupid?

   Tell myself I can do it.
   A one-person cheer team,
   that's what I am.

   You know I can't get a good word
   from his royal highness.

SONJA You don't need his—

LING No, I don't.

(*Pause*)

   But—

   well—

   it would be—

   no,
   you are right.
   I don't need it.

SONJA So
   that's why you joined the Red Guards
   because you didn't get Master Hua's—

LING No.

   I joined the Red Guards
   because I believed in
   their ideology of equality.

SONJA But your destruction of books and art—

LING We have no choice but to burn them.
They glorify and support
the old and oppressive ways.

Which country in the world
can boast of a truer democracy
where its youth takes an active part
in leading a nation?

Beat.

SONJA If the Red Guards demanded
the death of your father—

LING That's absurd—

SONJA If they did—

LING For what reason?—

SONJA If Master Hua represented the "old and
oppressive ways"—

LING I—

SONJA What would you do?

Beat.

LING That will never happen.

Sonja takes out a cigarette.

LING May I have one?

SONJA Cigarette?

Ling nods. Sonja gives Ling a cigarette. Ling studies the way Sonja holds her cigarette and imitates her. Sonja lights her lighter. Ling reaches to light her cigarette.

21

Back stage.

Ling is reading from a piece of paper.

Hua sits, tapping his foot.

An extremely long silence.

Hua gets up and walks near Ling, looking at her.

Hua walks back to his chair and sits.

HUA   So
        what did they say?

LING   You cannot perform
        The White-Haired Damsel
        anymore.

HUA   Why?

LING   It has been officially modified.

HUA   Modified into what?

LING   A ballet.

HUA   A ballet?
        The chairman's wife.
        Right?

LING   Yes.
        Jiang Qing.

        She also rewrote the story.

        The White-Haired Damsel
        cannot be raped by a landlord
        if she's to be a revolutionary.
        The White-Haired Damsel

will now resist him successfully
and bear no child.

HUA   At least
the cow has turned to writing.
Her acting was terrible.

I remember seeing her in that dreary—

LING   You shouldn't say such things aloud.
People may hear.

HUA   What people?

LING   People.
Just don't.

HUA   I knew I should have emigrated
when I had the—

LING   The Chairman's wife
has done away with all theater.

Beat.

HUA   All theater?

LING   All.

Except her model dramas.

Pause.

HUA   Model dramas?
What model dramas?

Ling reads from a paper.

LING   Every action,
every word,
every bar of music

in the play
must dramatize the class struggle—

HUA   Now,
she's the state censor.
Maybe I spoke too soon,
she should have stuck to acting—

LING   The hero of the play
must take the side of the proletariat
against the bourgeoisie—

HUA   Oh god,
do I have to play peasant girls from now on?—

LING   Also,
the hero must be fully integrated
into the masses
and boundlessly loyal to Chairman Mao—

HUA   My beautiful embroidered gowns!
What am I do with them!—

LING   All plays will be banned—

HUA   All plays?

LING   All plays
except for her five sanctioned model operas.

There will be severe consequences
for anyone
caught performing anything else—

HUA   My dear,
there is a lesson in all of this.

If you fail miserably
as a second-rate actress,

take up politics.
You'll find yourself
on yet a bigger stage.

Pause.

LING Papa,
you have to learn the model dramas.

HUA No.

LING You are not still planning
to perform the old operas?—

HUA Till I die.

LING But the consequences—

HUA What will I do?
Tell me—

LING They will arrest you —

HUA Ling,
look at me.
What will I do?
What else can I do?—

LING Learn the model plays—

HUA They are not plays!
They are written for the Chairman's wife.
Let her perform them!—

LING Papa!
Stop being stubborn!

Hua grabs Ling's hands and brings them to his face.

HUA Look.

Look.

Look at my face.

Feel it.
Every line.
Every crack.
Every pore.

For more than fifty years,
the greasy face paint,
the powders
have long seeped into my skin.
They are a part of me.
And I will die
with the paint and powders
still swimming in my blood.
And you think I want to?
You think I love coming in here
every day and every night,
putting on costumes,
singing, dancing
in front of loud, obnoxious,
unappreciative audiences?

I was sold
to the opera school
at the age of six,
because your grandfather,
a poor day laborer,
did not have enough money
to feed his entire family.
Being the youngest of seven sons,
he knew I was the most expendable.

I can never forget what he said to me.
"Aren't you a lucky one?
You're going to be on stage.
You're going to be an actor."
He said all this without any emotion,
any tears,
any concern.
His legacy to me.

All the while,
he fiercely dug his rough chapped hands
into mine.
Dragging me into the city
with uneven footsteps.
His breath
stinking of cheap wine.

I wanted to tell him.
I didn't want to be an actor.
I didn't want to be on stage.
All I wanted was to be at home.
With him.
With mother.

But I didn't.

My father
later deposited me
behind the large stone walls of the school. Then
he stumbled out of the gates,
too busy
counting the shiny bronze yuan
in his hands,

too busy
to say a final good-bye
to me.

Instead of watching him
bleed into the cold shadows
of cobbled streets outside,
I turned
toward the harsh embrace
of the school.
My new home.

The master
soon replaced my father.
A strict disciplinarian,
he trained me.
Hard.
Vigorously.
Rigorously.

In the mornings,
together with a host of other children,
we sang
the whole canon of Chinese operas.
Sang them
at the top of our little lungs.
Trained our voices
to sing
like valiant warrior men.
To sing
like virtuous country maidens
and
holy goddesses from the neglectful heavens.
All this before I reached sixteen.

And on hot afternoons,
a punishing
gregarious routine of gymnastics.

We danced in formation,
in unison,
in rhythm,
in sync,
as one.

The master behind us,
beating time with his large walking stick,
rapping rapping rapping
on the concrete floor.

We leapt
jumped
turned
flew
up into the air,
down onto the ground,
creating a beautiful fantastical world
in front of our eyes
in our heads,
to escape
the cruel world:
a world
of children without childhoods,
children within
the suffocating four walls of the school.

Sometimes
we plied stones and sticks
to our bent arms and knobby legs.
Stretched them

until they hurt,
until we couldn't feel them.
Straighten out
what nature didn't.

And I hated every moment of it.
This hell.
This abomination.
Hated what my father did to me.
Selling me off to opera school.
Abandoning me.

But I learned.
To accept it.

And I learned to love it.

Now
I'm too old
to learn anything else!

(*Hua refers to the theater.*)

This is my life.

This.

Here.

This place.

(*Beat*)

Look.

Look.

Look.

(Beat)

> I will die here.

Hua walks to exit.

LING The Red Guards asked me questions
about you
today.

Hua stops in his tracks.

HUA What did you say?

LING Nothing.
Nothing much.

Hua continues to walk.

LING They asked me to join them.

Hua turns to Ling.

HUA Will you?

LING They talked about equality,
justice for the people,
food for the hungry and—

HUA Will you join them?

LING I don't know.

HUA You can't.

> After my tea,
> we'll rehearse again.

22

Back stage.

Dressed in a Red Guard uniform, Ling is on stage. She is burning books and papers in a metal bin of fire.

In the other corner, Sonja and Hua look at Ling.

HUA   First,
the Red Guards
denounced their parents,
their teachers.
Interrogated intellectuals,
imprisoned artists.

Beating them.
Killing them.

Now,
they are burning paintings,
literature,
books.

The entire country has gone mad.

SONJA   Well,
there are some books
I'd be happy to set fire to.

HUA   Whose books?
Yours?

Hua looks at Ling.

HUA   Look.

Look at Ling.

Maybe
there is some good
to the Cultural Revolution after all.

Ling has finally come to her senses
and given up her silly notions
of being an actor,
an artist.

I don't know why she kept trying.

SONJA   My god—
             you were punishing her—
             discouraging her from the opera—

HUA   It's too hard a life in the opera—

SONJA   All the rehearsals—

HUA   She should have been a teacher,
             a politician—

SONJA   All the time she was trying so hard—

HUA   A museum curator,
             a writer—

SONJA   It was all an act—

HUA   I only want the best for her!

Sonja stares at Hua.

SONJA   You don't want her on the stage.
             The only person
             you want to see on the stage is you.
             And no one else.

HUA   She would never had made it.

SONJA She took over the theatre.
She must have something—

HUA She didn't have it in her.
Didn't have the fire.

Pause.

SONJA If you have to choose
between the theater and your daughter,
which would you choose?

HUA That's easy.

SONJA Which?

HUA You mean you don't know?

Beat.

Ling stops burning things. She looks at a particular book with much interest.

HUA So
how is my book coming along?

SONJA It's not—
It's coming along slowly—

HUA Why haven't you completed it?
Are you slacking off?
Laziness?
Writer's block?

SONJA All I have are
mere fragments—
jigsaw pieces
that don't quite fit—
shards of stories
that don't make sense—

Ling pockets the book into her uniform and leaves.

HUA   Finish it.
        I want the world to remember me.

23.

Back stage.

Hua sits at the dressing table, reading a manuscript and smoking.

Ling enters and walks towards Hua. Ling takes his cigarette from him.

LING   You can't smoke here anymore.

HUA   Since when?

LING   Since we the people
        confiscated this theatre.

Hua extinguishes his cigarette unwillingly.

HUA   Ling,
        come with me.

LING   I'm not listening to you, Comrade Hua.
        And no matter you say,
        I'm going on.

HUA   No,
        you are not.

        Come home with me.
        At once.

LING   Try stopping me.

HUA   You are not doing that trash.

LING   I wrote that "trash."

HUA   You didn't write the opera.
       Chekhov did.

LING   It is an adaptation.
       My interpretation of *Uncle Vanya*.
       Set in revolutionary China—

HUA   It's a stupid opera—

LING   It's a revolutionary opera.
       It's a good opera.
       A necessary opera.

HUA   I didn't waste my precious time
       training you
       to do trash.

LING   So I'm trained
       for the sole benefit
       of doing your kind of trash.

HUA   What do you mean by that?

LING   Your opera is fluff!

       Silly legends
       about romance and unrequited love.
       Insipid stories
       about social degenerates
       like concubines and courtesans.
       Women taking their lives
       for meaningless relationships
       and insincere men.
       They degrade women.

       Of course,
       why shouldn't they?

They were written
and performed by men.
Like yourself!

HUA   And what's wrong with that?

LING   When the audiences leave the theater,
they think
your opera is the way of the world.

HUA   That's not my responsibility—

LING   But you see,
it is.

HUA   At least,
my theater doesn't force everyone in the city

to come to the revolutionary opera
they don't give a shit about—

LING   Stage Manager Kong!
Kong!
Come throw this rambling old fart out!

Silence.

Hua and Ling look offstage.

Hua smiles.

HUA   Despite your taking over the theater,
Kong still knows his loyalties

LING   I would be very careful
not to flaunt that information
if I were you, Comrade Hua.
You and Comrade Kong could be—

HUA   What do you mean—

LING   People may hear—

HUA   You wouldn't dare!

In all these years,
he's been like a father to you—

LING   More than you'd ever be.

(*Silence*)

You are distracting me.
I have to prepare for the show.

HUA   Ling,
come home with me now.
And I'll forget everything.

LING   Why can't you be happy for me, Papa?

Happy,
I have finally found
something to believe in.
A purpose, a reason
to wake up to each and every morning.

Happy,
with millions of shiny-faced youths,
I am changing
our antiquated attitudes of thinking,
our old ways of living,
forging a new country with ideals and hope.

Happy—

I'm in an opera,
in the lead part?

Happy
I wrote the opera.

118

Why is it so difficult?

You keep putting me down,
saying I'm no good,
I'm not ready,
I'm good for nothing.

But I'm good, Papa.
Really good.
In my own right.
On my own terms.

I'm good.

HUA   They promised you the theater
if you joined the Red Guards,
didn't they?
If you kept an eye on me,
if you informed on me.

LING   I saved your skin, Papa.
You would've been killed
if someone else kept an eye on you.

HUA   No, no.
It's more that.
You want the theater.
My theater.

LING   Not everything is about the theater.
Please leave.

HUA   You sold out.

LING   I would like you to leave now.

HUA   Ha!
You think you're an actor?

An artist?
You're not.
You're not even halfway there.
You're useless!
You're nothing!

LING See?
The door over there?
Use it!

HUA Don't tell me what to do!

LING Leave!

HUA This is still my theater!

LING Not anymore!

Silence.

HUA You joined the Red Guards
because you wanted my theater.

And nothing else.

Beat.

LING The government
has taken over this establishment.
This is now
the People's theater
and we're doing plays
for the people.

And not plays
to indulge the fantasies
and whims of deluded actors.

You are a thing of the past.

Hua slaps Ling across the face.

Silence.

HUA Ling, I'm—

Hua tries to reach out to Ling, but she violently shrugs off his touch.

LING You are in my way.
I have an entrance to make.

Ling exits, leaving Hua behind.

Music transition.

During the transition, Ling grabs a stick and Hua puts a gunnysack over his head. This is reminiscent of the last scene in act 1.

Sonja tries to physically stop Ling and Hua but they ignore her.

SONJA No!

Ling, not—!
Please stop this—!

Don't!
Not again—
not—

(*Softly*)

Don't.

24.

On stage.

Hua is lying on the floor in a pool of light.

Ling takes the sack off Hua's head.

Sonja watches from back stage.

HUA   Tea—

LING   Papa.

HUA   I want some tea—
thirsty—
my throat—

LING   Papa,
I can't get any tea for you.
It's not possible.

HUA   Hmm.

LING   Papa,
are you?—

HUA   I—
think they broke—
something.

LING   They gave me a few minutes with you.

Hua groans.

HUA   Ahh—

LING   Pain there?

HUA   No—
all over.

Silence.

LING   Papa,
you should have emigrated
when you had the chance.
To Europe.
To America.

122

HUA   You think—
      they'll take me?

LING You were a sensation.
      You told me.

HUA   A sensation?
      During the tour—
      one night—
      I slipped off to a theater—
      in New York—
      without my hosts—
      Spent the evening—
      watching a play—

(*Coughs*)

      A play about a man—
      his life unlived—
      At the end—
      he sits with his niece—

LING Yes—

HUA   Two of them—
      sitting in a cold room—
      dreaming of a better—
      a brighter life ahead—
      Now what did she say?—

LING "We must go on living.
      We shall go on living, Uncle Vanya.
      We shall live—"

HUA   Yes—
      I was so—
      captivated—

so moved—
by what I saw.

Hua has a coughing fit.

LING Shh.
Don't talk anymore—

HUA After the show—
I walked into the foyer—
walked amongst the crowd—
no one—no one looked at me—
as if I was air—
invisible—
ahhh—

Hua winces in pain.

LING Papa—

HUA But these were the same people—
the same people—
who had come to see me the week before
when I was on stage—
but—
without my costumes—
my songs—
I was nothing—
Faceless
in the sea of faces.

Beat.

HUA You know—what I'd love?—

LING Tea?—

HUA The way—
I like it—

LING I'll go get you some—

An emotional Ling doesn't move.

HUA Tea—

LING Yes—

HUA Hot—

LING Yes—

HUA Tea—

LING The way you like it—

HUA And Ling?—
Sing—
sing me that song—

LING That we used to sing?—

HUA Yes—
the one we used to sing right here—

Slowly and with much difficulty, Ling sings very slowly and softly.

LING "Gently, gently
She dances to her father's voice
Gently, gently
In *mei hua* blossom night

Gently, gently—"

Hua dies.

Silence.

Ling is about to cry but restrains her emotions.

She looks up into the balcony.

LING   Someone help get him off me!
The class enemy is dead!

25.

Back stage.

As in the last scene, Hua's lifeless body is lying on top of Ling.

Sonja enters.

LING   Did you spell my name correctly?

SONJA   For the last time,
yes.

LING   I just want to make sure
you've gotten all the facts.
All the details.
About what happened.
What truly happened.
I'm not responsible for my father's—

SONJA   You've said that already—

LING   I want to be clear.
I want you to know everything.
Everything that happened.

I'm not responsible—

SONJA   I know.

Beat.

LING   How many people,
do you think,
will read this book?

SONJA So,
what happened to your father?

Hua slowly gets up and exits.

LING He was—
purged.

His death was officially classified
a suicide.

SONJA But it was murder.

LING It was—
suicide.

SONJA If you say so.
Then what happened?

LING I took flight.
In 1976,
when Chairman Mao
finally died of a long illness,
the government splintered into factions.

Soon,
the Communist Party officials denounced
Jiang Qing and the Gang of Four
as counterrevolutionaries.

SONJA Ironic.

LING And the Cultural Revolution
was declared obsolete,
a national mistake—

SONJA A mistake!
Lives and art were meaninglessly destroyed!
And it was all a mistake!

127

LING   So I left—

SONJA   Because
you knew
you'd be prosecuted by the new regime—

LING   Yes—
I'd be killed for—

SONJA   For the murders of your father—

LING   No—!

SONJA   And Stage Manager Kong
who took care of you—!

LING   I was not responsible!
I had to do it!

Don't you see?
I had to!—

SONJA   You wanted to be on the stage
at all costs!—

LING   No!

SONJA   Even at the expense of your father's life!—

LING   No!

Pause.

SONJA   Continue.

LING   I—
I packed a few things
and fled to the countryside.
Trying to get over to—

SONJA Hong Kong—

LING Yes—
it was unsafe for me
to remain in China any longer—

SONJA It was a long and tiring journey—

LING Yes—
I walked for weeks from Shanghai—
the dirt roads were deserted, lonely—
the paddy fields were often shrouded in—

SONJA Fog and mists—

LING Yes—
Everything looked hazy and uncertain—
I stowed away—

SONJA In loud rattling trains—

LING And sometimes
I'd wearily walk alongside the—

SONJA Railroad tracks—
Yes—

LING Tracks lined with plum trees—

SONJA No—
Not plum—
Mei hua—
Mei hua blossom trees—
They were—

LING You're right—
Of course–
Mei hua blossom trees—
I—

SONJA   Walked for days—
        I had no—

LING   Food and water—
        and finally I reached—

SONJA   The South China Sea—
        Yes—
        Remember?—

LING   Yes—

SONJA   I swam—
        In the icy black waters—
        Choppy, strong—

LING   I was so tired—
        Water was—

SONJA   Cold—
        I thought I couldn't make it—

LING   Have to *ren*—

SONJA   *Ren*—

LING   Endure—

SONJA   And I swam on—

LING   Remember the cold?—

SONJA   Yes—
        Cold—

LING   I felt I was ripped into two—

SONJA   Finally—
        when I thought I wasn't going to—

LING   I finally reached the other side!—

SONJA   I collapsed on the sandy beach—
dragged—

LING   My heavy body
into the forest unnoticed—

SONJA   And stayed there—

LING   Till it was safe
to go into the city.

Beat.

SONJA   Later,
I would change my name—

Ling walks to Sonja.

LING   From Ling—

SONJA   To Sonja.

LING   After the niece in the Chekhov play,
Uncle Vanya.

Ling reaches to touch Sonja's face but Sonja shies away.

LING   Sonja Wong Pickford.

SONJA   Famous writer.

(*Softly*)

I hate you.

Why did you kill him?

Why?

Why?

LING You know why

Ling walks off.

26.

Back stage.

Hua is sitting at his table putting on makeup. His back is toward the audience throughout this scene.

SONJA Papa,
I'm sorry.

HUA For what?

SONJA I—
can't write the book.

HUA Why?

SONJA The book won't come to me.
Somehow,
the book just won't come to me.
The stories,
the words don't add up.

They are lonely,
isolated pieces.
Pieces out of sequence,
out of joint,
out of time.
Pieces
that never amount
to the full picture.

I hardly knew you.

HUA Find it in the silence.
Find it in the cracks.
Find it in the details.

SONJA I can't.
I see nothing.

I spent
half of my life
trying to forget China.
Trying to forget you
and all that happened.

HUA Then
why did you want
to unleash the past?
Why did you want to come back here?

SONJA I—don't know.

HUA Oh, you know.

SONJA What are you—?

HUA You want to write "Something more.
Something important.
Something big.
Something credible."

You want to use my life
and your past,
no matter how painful
and difficult.

SONJA No—

HUA It's all right.
I don't care.

After all, it's only a story.

133

SONJA   It's not only a story.
          It's my life!

(*Beat*)

          If I remember anything vividly,
          I remember this theater.

          This dreadful theater
          where everything happened.

HUA   You have to *ren*.

SONJA   Yes.
          Of course.
          Ren.
          Your answer to everything.

HUA   It helps.

SONJA   It doesn't!

          Every time,
          I lie in bed,
          I keep thinking
          if I could've done something—

HUA   Something heroic?—

SONJA   Done something to save you—
          I could have spoken up—
          I could have—

HUA   You could have done nothing—
          They were bigger than you were—
          You'd have been swallowed up—

SONJA   Instead I succumbed—
          yielded—

I could have—
something—
something—

HUA You'd have been killed—
ended up the same way I did—

SONJA You don't know that!—

HUA You don't know anything!—

SONJA Don't dismiss me!—

HUA You know nothing!—

SONJA Stop directing me
like one of your characters
in your stupid operas!

HUA You're still that misguided ignorant girl!—

SONJA If I did—
if I did something!—

HUA Oh,
and everything would be perfect!—

SONJA Yes!
Everything would be perfect!—

HUA I did what was best for you!

Long pause.

SONJA Best for me?

Did you know
I've been having nightmares?
Recurring nightmares
of both of us

in this theater
for past twenty-five years?

I sleep in this theater every night!

And every night,
I wondered
if I could change my lines,
change the outcome of the scene.

But every night,
the actress is line perfect,
she knows her cues,
her blocking.

Nothing changes,
and why should it?
She's been taught
by the best acting teacher
in the business.

HUA   You're alive.
It's all that matters.

SONJA You made me denounce you.
Made me participate
in the senseless,
ruthless killings.

What kind of person—
What kind of child—
would do that?

HUA   An obedient child.

A child
who listened to her father.

A child
who loved her father.

Hua looks at Sonja for a long moment.

HUA Sometimes
things are never the way
you want them to be.

One day
you wake up
and you realize
all that you believed in
was wrong,
all the good you thought you did was detrimental.
Time can do that to you.

The flag
you give your life for,
suddenly hates you.
A child
you think you know,
turns into a stranger.

So,
you do either of two things:
You fight with it,
and lose that inevitable war.

Or,
you hold its cold hands,
and pray.

HUA What are you going to do?

Beat.

Ling appears.

Sonja motions for Ling to take off her Red Guard uniform. Ling hands her uniform to Sonja. Sonja dresses in Ling's uniform.

After Sonja has finished dressing, she looks at Ling. Ling looks at Sonja.

27.

On stage.

Sonja in a Red Guard uniform. Her demeanor and tone is that of Ling's in the prior scenes.

Hua holds up a play.

SONJA   So
        you admit you wrote this opera!

HUA   Yes,
        I wrote the Chekhov opera.

SONJA   Your opera is counterrevolutionary!
        In black and white.
        On page forty-six!
        You insinuate—

HUA   I insinuate nothing!
        You have completely misinterpreted
        the good intentions
        of this worthy opera!

SONJA (*Whispering*)   Papa,
        I won't do this anymore.
        I won't—

HUA (*Whispering*)   You must—
        I will take the responsibility—

SONJA (*Whispering*)   You won't—
　　　　　　there will be severe consequences—

HUA (*Out*)   You're seeing
　　　　　what you've chosen to see
　　　　　in this work of art!

　　　　　You have twisted
　　　　　every innocent word of the opera
　　　　　to further your own political agenda
　　　　　and ambitions!

SONJA   Shut up!
　　　I'm not here to play games with you!

HUA   Neither am I!
　　　I've done nothing wrong!

SONJA   Jiang Qing condemns your opera!

HUA   I insist you release me at once!

SONJA (*Whispering*)   Papa,
　　　　　　I will confess.

HUA (*Whispering*)   I said
　　　　　I'll take the blame for your opera—

SONJA (*Whispering*)   No, you won't—
　　　　　　I will confess—

HUA (*Whispering*)   You will not—

SONJA (*Whispering*)   This has gone on long enough, Papa—

Sonja grabs the play from Hua and stands in front of him. She looks out into the house.

HUA   Ling—

139

SONJA Hey!
You!
Up there!

HUA Ling, what are you doing?

SONJA I have a confession!
I confess!
It was me!—

HUA No!
It was me!
I was responsible for the Chekhov opera!—

SONJA I authored the Chekhov opera!–

HUA I wrote it!

SONJA And it was a good revolutionary opera!
It exalted
all of Chairman Mao's teachings!—

HUA She doesn't know
what she's talking about!
It was me!—

SONJA Everything
was taken from Mao's book!
Every single word!—

HUA I wrote it!

SONJA And
it was infinitely better
than Jiang Qing's so-called operas!—

HUA I wrote it!—
It was me!—

SONJA No,
it was me!

HUA It was me!—

SONJA Me!—

HUA Me!—

SONJA Me!

Silence.

SONJA No.

HUA He's not there.

SONJA No.

HUA He's gone.

SONJA No.

Pause.

SONJA Papa,
I didn't know it would turn out like this.
I thought
the Red Guards was going to be—
it's all a mistake—
My mistake.

HUA I know, Ling.

I don't want to talk about it anymore.

SONJA I'll quit from the Red Guards—

HUA Are you stupid?

They will immediately
become suspicious
if you leave the Red Guards.

Any sudden change of heart
will arouse their curiosity.
And they'll come straight for you.

You stay with them,
through the bitter end.

SONJA   I'll tell them the truth—

HUA   Think,
Ling,
think.

They've already targeted me
as an artist.
The Chekhov opera
is just another charge
they will stack against me.

This Cultural Revolution nonsense
will not last forever.
They will have to release me eventually.

SONJA   What if they don't?

What if they kill you?

HUA   And you think
your truth is going to save me?

After they've purged you,
don't you think
they'll do the same to me?
What will be left of us?
Our family?
What will be left of all
that I have taught you?
My legacy.

Is that what you want?
What's wrong with you?

You are
all I have.

Please,
Ling.

For the last time,
do as I say.

Sonja kneels on the floor.

SONJA Papa. I'm sorry.

HUA I know, Ling.
I know.

Now,
get up.
Get up
before they see you.

Sonja does not get up. Hua kneels beside Sonja.

HUA You know
I'll be out of here soon.

SONJA Yes—
when you get out of here—

HUA We'll go home—
celebrate—
have a feast—

SONJA Forget all of this—

HUA And we'll come back to the theater—

SONJA You can act again—

HUA None of those revolutionary dramas—

SONJA *The White-Haired Damsel*—

HUA I think you're ready—

I saw your performance
in that dreadful Chekhov opera you wrote—

SONJA On stage with you—

HUA Oh no.
I'm too old.

I'm history.

SONJA You're not.

HUA It's your turn now.

Go.
Go make history.

Sonja and Hua stand.

Sonja looks out into the audience.

SONJA He's back.

I see him.

I don't know if I can—

HUA Yes.
You can.

You're an actress.

Let the scene begin.

Hua holds up the confession paper as he did at the top of scene 18.

EPILOGUE

Sonja changes from her Red Guard uniform back into her original outfit.

SONJA   Story of my life.

There I was.
At the height of my career.
Swimming in a swamp of
parties,
papparazzi,
press,
and personalities.

I'm an author.
Sonja Wong Pickford.
You may have heard of me.

If you haven't,
visit your local bookstore.
Check under "romance."
And
there I am.

After twenty years
in the business,
I was afraid to die,
and leave behind
a legacy of ethnic romances
to my name.

You see,
I wanted to write something more.
Something important.
Something big.
Something credible.

But
nothing came to me.

So,
I flew back,
to the arms of Shanghai,
after twenty-five years.

(*Beat*)

During my last week in Shanghai,
I was contacted by the Chinese government
inviting me to a banquet ceremony
in honor of my father,
Hua Wai Mun

The banquet was held
in a large antiseptic meeting hall.
Communist officials and artists
had gathered to commemorate
Papa's theatrical achievements and
accomplishments.

Some of them were Papa's fellow actors.
Swee Keong, Ming Yao, Keng Sen,
they were all there.
I remembered
some of the crusty old farts
from the old days.

Also,
in the room,
were some of Papa's colleagues
who delivered false testimonies
against him
during the Cultural Revolution.

But all of them
came up to congratulate me.
Said they've all read
Bound Feet, Bound Lives
and loved it.

They even saw the television movie.

The old men and women
showered me
with a torrent of adjectives,
superlatives
about what a fine artist Papa was.

Some offered flowery words of flattery,
amusing anecdotes
stories of his influence on their lives.

They should have said something.
To him.
When he was alive.

When I pressed them
for more information on Papa,
they said nothing.
Shook their heads.
Smiled.
And walked away.

Papa would be very pleased.

The banquet served roast pig.

(*Beat*)

But,
for me,
the highlight of my trip
was my first day in Shanghai.

147

I had stumbled,
quite by accident
onto the path home,
the opera theater
where I had spent my youth.

I had forgotten where it was.

As if guided by old memories,
by Papa's indomitable spirit,
I found it.

There.

On Unity Road.

The theater greeted me warmly
as a wrinkled old friend would.

It looked shyly abandoned.
Unused.
Silent.
It didn't seem to recognize me.

Ling enters carrying a suitcase.

Sonja does not acknowledge her throughout this scene.

LING   I spent a long time
            in the darkened empty theater—

SONJA   Spent most of the afternoon
            in the dressing room—

LING   Where Papa smoked endless cigarettes—

SONJA   Drank endless cups of tea—

Sonja and Ling sniff the air.

LING I could still smell
        the faint scent of makeup powder—

SONJA Could still smell Papa,
        in the theater—

LING I must have dozed off.

        I found my head
        resting on the dressing table
        when I awoke.

        Groggy from my sleep,
        I was enveloped by
        the cold caress of night air—

SONJA I tugged my overcoat around me tightly—

LING And made my way
        out of the theater—

SONJA (*Sadly*) I know I'll never return.

LING (*Excitedly, optimistically*) Never.
                        I'll never come back.

Beat.

SONJA As I was climbing down from the stage,
        a tune,
        a fractured melody,
        trickled into my consciousness.

        A song.

        No—

Hua enters and looks at Sonja and Ling who do not notice him.
Hua sings the lullaby.

LING   A lullaby—

SONJA   A lullaby—

LING   That Papa used to sing to me.

SONJA   How did it go?
That lullaby?
What was it?
"Gently, gently" something.

LING   No,
no more lullabies.

Ling reaches for her luggage.

SONJA   That lullaby.
I can't remember how it went.
I'm sure
it wasn't that important anyway.

(Leaves the tape recorder on the ground)

I made my way back home.

Sonja walks away.

Ling walks off the stage.

Sonja sits down and looks out into audience.

Hua walks slowly towards Sonja, singing the lullaby.

Sonja listens to the lullaby.

HUA   "Gently, gently
She dances to her father's voice
Gently, gently
in *mei hua* blossom night—"

"Gently, gently
Mei hua fades to winter white
The little girl child
She's no longer in sight

Gently, gently
Mei hua flower blossoms sway
Gently, gently
Her father misses her face"

In silence, Sonja lifts her hands and dances to the White-Haired
Damsel. *Hua, standing behind her, joins her. Both Hua and Sonja
dance in unison.*

Lights slowly fade to black.

THE END

SCISSORS

Soon-Tek Oh (A) and Arye Gross (B)
Photo: Craig Schwartz

Scissors was first presented in The Square in Los Angeles on June 29, 2000, at the Mark Taper Forum's Taper, Too; Gordon Davidson, artistic director.

A	Soon-Tek Oh
B	Ayre Gross
Director	Lisa Peterson
Set Design	Rachel Hauck
Costume Design	Joyce Kim Lee
Lighting Design	Geoff Korf
Original Music and Sound Design	Nathan Wang
Dramaturge	Chay Yew
Production Stage Manager	Erika H. Sellin

Scissors was originally commissioned
by the Mark Taper Forum's Asian Theatre Workshop.

Scissors is for Ayre Gross and Soon-Tek Oh.

SCISSORS

1929, one month after the crash.

A park in Chinatown, New York.

A is an Asian man in his seventies. He is blind.

B is a Caucasian man in his seventies and is dressed in a black suit.

B sits on a park bench, holding his walking cane, while A stands behind him, cutting his hair with a pair of scissors.

A   Mister Richard?

B   Building.

A   Mister Derek.

B   Bridge.

A   Manhattan?

B   Brooklyn.

A   Ah I see. Mrs. Mathilda?

B   Gunshot wound.

A   Temple?

B   No. Mouth.

A   Fitting end. That one always had big mouth.

B   Yes. Remember how she ordered you around to fetch her things?—

A   "Boy, fetch my mink stole—"

B   "Boy, fetch my smelling salts—"

A "Boy, fetch my necklace—"

B "Boy, fetch my husband—"

A and B laugh. Beat.

A Mrs. Mathilda dead. Sometimes there is God.

B No, not God. Stock market.

Pause.

A You?

B What do you mean?

A Stock market.

Pause.

B I'm fine—

A What do you mean "fine?"—

B I'm fine—

A Sir, is there something I should know?—

B You don't have to call me "sir" anymore.

A Habit.

B I know, George.

A George not my name.

B I gave you that name.

A Because you never can remember my real name.

B What do they call you here?

A Nothing. They no speak to me here. I stranger here.

Silence, except for the snip snip of the scissors.

A   You invest?

B   What are you talking about?

A   Stock market. You invest?

B   Yes.

A   And?

B   I'm fine. The company's—unscratched.

A   I no worry about you. But your children.
Monsters. They never listen to you. Always
try to take away your company—

B   Everything's fine. I'm fine. Stop nagging, okay?

A   Okay.

Silence, except for the snip snip of the scissors.

B   Look, in fact, I made out like a bandit in the
crash. To celebrate, I went straight to Beau
Brummel and bought myself a new red suit. I'm
wearing it right now.

A feels B's black suit.

A   Red suit?

B   It's the latest fashion to Charleston in.

A   What is this Charleston?

B   A dance in four-four time. It's the rage all
over the world.

A   Dancing at your age?

159

B hums a rapid melodious tune and pretends to dance the Charleston while sitting down.

A (*Laughing*)   Stop! Stop! Stop! You getting senile!

B   You should see the suit! It's dapper!

A   I blind. (*Beat*) I would love to see you dance Charleston.

B   It's quite a sight.

A   Maybe you teach me Charleston.

B   Sure. I can teach it to you.

A   We can do it here.

B   Where everyone can see.

A   It will be quite a sight.

Silence, except for the snip snip of the scissors.

A   How they treating you? The monsters.

B   Like a child. Can't do this. Can't do that. The only thing they allow me to do, on my own, is to take the tram here every Sunday—

A   The tram? You say Harold take you—

B   Did I say the tram? I meant to say that they allow me to use the driver on Sundays. I *am* getting senile. How about your monsters?

A   The same. They work too hard. Sometimes I help out at their provision shop on Bayard Street. What little I can. I know they want me out of way. They say "Ah Pa, you spend whole life working, now time for you to relax, slow down." Which mean you too old, you blind, get out of way. Funny, these children first need you all the time. Now suddenly, they don't need you anymore. If I relax, slow down, I will die.

B   I know the feeling.

Silence, except for the snip snip of the scissors.

A   They looking over here again?

B   Yes.

A   You know, I give them something to talk about. Blind Chinaman cutting *gwai loh*'s hair right in middle of Columbus Park.

B   You don't have to cut my hair.

A   I need to.

Silence, except for the snip snip of the scissors.

B   You know, I go to sleep hearing this.

A   Hearing what?

B   This. The snip snips of your scissors. The tiny snip snips. Precise. Clean. The endless restless murmur of metal blades. It immediately comforts me. Forces me surrender my body, my soul, to the serenity of the snip snips. Makes me drift away from this world. Surface in another quite unlike this one.

Snip snip of the scissors.

B   Snip snip. Snip snip. Can you hear it? What sounds do you sleep to?

A Yelling, laughing. Drunk people in saloon
   across the street. Click clack click clack
   sound of mah-jonng tiles next door. Screaming
   screaming. Children running up down up down
   the road.

B You know you can come back and live with me—

A Silly fool. Your monsters, my monsters won't
   like. A Chinaman living with you. It upset their
   world.

B I can speak to them.

A You don't understand. It no longer our world.

Silence, except for the snip snip of the scissors.

B Oh, listen. Do you need any money? I've got
   some—

A I okay.

B digs into his pockets, fishes out a wallet and takes out some money.

B Here take some—

A I say I okay—

B Take it—

A No—

B I want you to have it—

A I have enough. You keep it.

B Take—

*A slaps the bills out of B's hand. A immediately goes down on his
knees feeling the ground for the money. B looks at A for several beats.*

B helps A to pick up the money. A finds the money and thrusts the bills back to B's hands.

A and B resume their routine.

Silence, except for the snip snip of the scissors.

B I'm sorry.

A It's okay.

B It's not. I always—

A I know.

B I just want you to be–

A I know.

A pats B on the shoulder.

A I know.

A resumes cutting B's hair. Suddenly A winces in pain.

A Ouch!

B What's wrong?

A Cut myself.

B Let me see.

B takes A's hand into his own.

A It's okay.

B Let me take a look at it.

A It's okay. Really.

B places his mouth over A's cut, licking his wound tenderly. A is still.

A They looking.

B They are not looking.

A I see them looking.

B Let them look.

A I live here. You don't.

B Iron.

A What?

B Your blood. It tastes like iron.

Slowly B withdraws his mouth from A's hand. A's hand makes a slow and deliberate study of B's face.

A You getting old.

B Is that a fact?

A I miss feeling your face.

B Yes.

A Different, but yet still same. The same.

B They're looking.

A Let them look.

A slowly retrieves his hand and starts cutting B's hair again.

Silence, except for the snip snip of the scissors.

B looks at his watch.

A What time?

B About five.

A Five.

Silence, except for the snip snip of the scissors.

B I should get going.

A So soon?

B I've got a board meeting early tomorrow
morning.

A Board meeting?

B Correspondences to catch up on. Product meetings
to organize. So on and so forth.

Silence, except for the snip snip of the scissors.

A You should stop working. At your age. Work
yourself to—

B I know. I know.

Silence, except for the snip snip of the scissors.

B There's Harold.

B waves to no one. Everyone in the park looks at him bewilderedly.

B He's waving to me. It's time to go.

B calls out to no one.

B In a moment, Harold!

A Harold the driver?

B Yes.

A Harold still working for you?

B Yes.

A Really?

B Really.

Pause.

A   Call him over.

B   Some other time.

A   I want to say hello to him.

B   Some other time.

A   No, I want to—

B   I said some other time!

Pause.

A   Okay. Some other time.

Silence.

A   See you next week?

B   Yes. Of course.

Silence.

A   Sunday.

B   For another trim.

A   Yes.

Silence.

B   Sunday.

A   Sunday.

Both A and B don't move. After a long while, A resumes to cut B's hair.

Snip snip of the scissors.

THE END

A BEAUTIFUL
COUNTRY

Chris Wells, Nancy Yee, Eric Steinberg, José Casas, and
Gwendolyn Yeo
Photo: Craig Schwartz

A Beautiful Country was first presented in Los Angeles on June 5, 1998, at the Cornerstone Theater Company; Bill Rauch, artistic director.

Company	Chu Kiet Au
	José Casas
	Tina Chao
	Reggie Lee
	Page Leong
	Armando Molina
	Jeanne Sakata
	Eric Steinberg
	Jessica Wallenfels
	Christopher S. Wells
	John Lung Wen
	Nancy Yee
	Gwendoline Yeo
Director	Chay Yew
Set Design	Akeime Mitterlehner
Costume Design	Ann Closs-Farley
Lighting Design	Geoff Korf
Original Music and Sound Design	Nathan Wang
Choreography	Jessica Wallenfels
Dramaturges	Peter Tamaribuchi,
	Amy Vaillancourt
Production Stage Manager	Victoria Gathe

Some portions of *A Beautiful Country* are inspired by, incorporate, use, or are taken from newspapers, journals, literature, historical documents, and interviews.

A Beautiful Country was originally commissioned by Cornerstone Theatre Company.

A Beautiful Country is for Luis Alfaro.

A BEAUTIFUL COUNTRY

A simple set.

There is a raised platform at the center of the stage; this is the acting area.

The actors, dancers, and musicians sit on chairs on the side of the acting area.

There is a standing microphone stage left. A video monitor on stage right. These are never moved during the play.

PRESET

When the house is open, a video of the restless roaring blue ocean is projected on the cyclorama.

A soundtrack of ocean waves, interviews with local Chinatown residents in Cantonese and Mandarin, and VISA's *voice uttering different passages from this play is heard.*

On stage, there is a lit blue square.

A.

Fluorescent lights.

Upstage spot on the IMMIGRATION OFFICER, *a Caucasian man in his thirties or forties.*

Downstage spot on Visa who is dressed like Madonna. His back is against the audience.

OFFICER   Passport please
Passport

Name?

Purpose of this trip
Purpose
Why are you here?
Business?
Pleasure?
Working?
Vacation?

I see

How long will you be here?

How long?
Days?
Weeks?
Months?
You cannot stay
for more than three months

You don't know
I see

Let me see your return ticket
Ticket
Plane ticket
Yes
that blue folder

(*Visa holds out his hand.*)

No return
I see

You cannot stay
for more than three months

What do you do for a living in—
What do you—
Occupation
Job
Work

Hairdresser
I see

Can you demonstrate—
show me—
the funds
you have for this trip?

Funds

Money

Yen
You have money?
Cash?
Travelers checks?

Yes
American Express
Show me

(*Visa holds out his hand.*)

You know
You cannot stay
for more than three months

(*Officer picks up phone, mutters into it and then hangs up.*)

Can you step out of the line?

(*Visa gets up from his table.*)

Come
here
We have some questions to ask you

(SECURITY GUARDS *to escort Visa.*)

Please follow these officers
Follow them
follow them
to the next room

Next

B.

A traditional shadow play.

In a cappella, a SINGER sings a traditional Chinese railroad song.

Behind a silk fabric screen, CHINESE RAILROAD WORKERS are portrayed in their daily activities, i.e. coming to America via immigration, digging and hammering rivets on railroad tracks, prostitution, the deaths of dynamite runners, etc.

At the end of this scene, all the WORKERS fall down dead with the fabric screen above them.

C.

SLIDE: TESTIMONY

SLIDE: GWENDOLINE YEO

Gwendoline Yeo is a Chinese-Singaporean immigrant.

GWENDOLINE When I first arrived in America,
I was jetlagged confused excited,
all at once.

I remembered
stepping out of the airport
and feeling the cool California wind
touch my skin.
It was like stepping
into an air-conditioned room in
Singapore.
That's where I'm originally from.

I've been in the States
for nine years now,
but the first day
always sticks in my mind.

I remember
I was at a store
buying my school uniform.
I was trying on these little plaid
skirts
for Catholic school.
I looked over at my mom.
She was frowning really hard,
but she didn't realize how hard
she was frowning.
She had so many things to worry about.

See,
when we first came over here
from Singapore,

my dad,
who was a physician there,
had to start his residency from scratch.
My mom
she took on a minimum-wage job
selling sewing machines.
And I only had to worry
about being in seventh grade.

I had glasses,
I wore braces,
and I had this awful British accent
a lot of kids have
when they come over
from Hong Kong or Singapore.
I was basically
a geek.

When I was in high school,
things didn't get much easier.
Race became more and more of an issue.
My American friends were like,
"Why are you hanging with
those Asian gangsters?"
And my Asian friends where like,
"Why do you hang out with
those blondies?"
I used to get to school
two minutes before the bell rang
so I wouldn't have
to choose.

But when I was sixteen,
things began to really change for me.

My body
was finally catching up
to the rest of my early-blooming
classmates.
I had a boyfriend
who really adored me.
And I skipped senior prom
to do something else.
Something
that would mean a lot more to me.
Something
that would value
the color of my skin
and the color of my hair–
black hair, black eyes.
And something
that would value my ethnic heritage.

I joined the pageant.
The Miss Teen Chinatown San Francisco
Pageant.

I'm glad I skipped prom,
because I happened to win too.

After that,
things started to really get rolling
for me.

My entire family started to move on.
My dad is a full professor now
and he's a practicing doctor.
My mom gets more and more beautiful
each day,
and she's now an RDA.

My sister is in medical school
and my brother just finished a Ph.D.
at Cambridge in molecular genetics.

And then
there's me.
I was very honored
this February to win the title of
Miss Chinatown USA 1998.

It was like an Academy Award
for this
young, dirty Chinese immigrant kid
finally coming into her own.

D.

MC Ladies and gentlemen
Miss Visa Denied!

*Visa and DANCERS come out. They lip-synch and dance to
Madonna's "Vogue."*

E.

SLIDE: October 24, 1871

SLIDE: Los Angeles

*In silence and through movement, an actor physically enacts the entire
massacre from all different points of view that ends in a hanging.*

*After the actor is "hanged," a Chinese song about homesickness will
be sung a cappella.*

SLIDE: Just three blocks
south from here

SLIDE: Negro Alley

SLIDE: Now known as Los
Angeles Street,
situated in the
heart of the Plaza,
near Olvera
Street

SLIDE: A white Angeleno
was killed during
an arrest of a
Chinese

SLIDE: News of the attack
spread like
wildfire throughout
the city

SLIDE: An armed mob of 500
rushed to Negro
Alley

SLIDE: A five-hour orgy of
rioting, looting,
and murder ensued

SLIDE: Police made no
attempt to arrest the rioters

SLIDE: By the evening's
end, nineteen lives would
be lost

SLIDE: At the corner of
Los Angeles and
Commercial Streets

SLIDE: and the corner of
Temple and
New High Streets

SLIDE: hung fifteen Chinese men

SLIDE: four more were shot
and stabbed to
death

SLIDE: In a trial after
the massacre, seven men
would be found
guilty.

SLIDE: Their convictions
were reversed on
appeal and they
were set free

SLIDE: Under California
law, the Chinese
were not
permitted to
testify in matters
involving
Caucasians

F.

SLIDE: 1879

SLIDE: AN EXCERPT

SLIDE: HENRY GRIMM'S *THE CHINESE MUST GO*

Vaudeville theatre style. Strip lights. Backdrop.

MC Ladies and gentlemen,
and now
an exerpt
from Henry Grimm's play
The Chinese Must Go!

SAM GIN *is washing dishes.*

AH COY *is smoking his opium pipe.*

AH COY I tellee you,
white man big fools;
eaty too muchee,
drinkee too muchee,
and talkee too muchee.

SAM GIN White man catchee plentee money;
Chinaman catchee little money.

AH COY By and by white man catchee no money;
Chinaman catchee heap money;
Chinaman workee cheap, plenty work;
white man workee dear, no work—
sabee?

SAM GIN Me heep sabee.

AH COY White man damn fools;
keep wifee and children
cost plenty money;
Chinaman no wife, no children,
save plenty money.
By and by,

no more white workingman in California;
all Chinaman—
sabee?

FRANK BLAINE *enters.*

FRANK Damn such luck;
can't borrow a cent to save my life.
Money is getting
as scarce as flies about Christmas.

I must have some.

Losing three games of billiards,
one after another,
with this flat-footed Jack Flint
is a shame.

(*To Ah Coy*)

Why don't you work?

AH COY Your mother no payee me last month;
no payee, no workee—
sabee?

FRANK How much does she owe you?

AH COY Six dollars.

FRANK All right, John;
I get it for you.

(*Aside*)

If I squeeze the six dollars
out of the old man
that Chinaman has to pay me commission,
that's business.

Frank pulls Sam Gin by his queue. Sam Gin shrieks. Frank exits.

SAM GIN Damn hoodlum!
What for you foolee me
all the time?

LIZZIE *enters.*

LIZZIE Has my brother been here, John?

SAM GIN Your brother damn hoodlum,
he pullee my tail all the time.

LIZZIE They are all trying to send you
back to China, John.
Oh, how nervous I am this morning.

AH COY You like smoke opium?

LIZZIE Yes, please.

Lizzie takes the opium pipe and inhales. Ah Coy smells her body and licks her arm.

AH COY Drinkee too much coffee;
no good,
makee too muchee shaking—
sabee?

WILLIAM BLAINE *enters and takes the pipe out of his daughter's mouth.*

WILLIAM What!
Are you smoking this dirty pipe again?

(*Kicking Ah Coy*)

WILLIAM Get out of my house,
you miserable dog.

AH COY I wantee money.

WILLIAM Take that!

(*Striking Ah Coy with the pipe*)

You breeder of ruin and desolation.

AH COY I make you pay.

Ah Coy exits.

DORA *enters.*

DORA What's this noise about?
What's the matter?

WILLIAM The matter is
that you are too damned fond
of sitting in the parlor yourself
in the chair
and reading trash
instead of looking after
your household affairs.

There,
I caught our girl again smoking
that nasty Chinaman's pipe.

DORA Poor thing!
She is sick.

WILLIAM Is it a wonder?
She has nothing else to do
but to get sick.

I told you a thousand times,
why the devil don't you make her work?

DORA   Why the devil don't you make Frank work?

WILLIAM   Haven't I been hunting for a place
for years?

Isn't every factory and every store
crammed with
those cursed Chinamen?

DORA   Excuses!
Excuses!

LAM WOO *enters bringing washing.*

WILLIAM (*To Lam Woo*)   What do you want?

LAM WOO   Me bringing wash.

WILLIAM   Wash yourself to hell;
I've got no money.

LAM WOO   Your wife owe me sixteen dollars.
You no got money
I keepee washee.

Lam Woo exits.

WILLIAM   Sixteen dollars for washing!

William exits.

Ah Coy, Lam Woo and SLIM CHUNK PIN *enter.*

DORA   Thank heavens, my husband isn't here.

SLIM CHUNK PIN   Madam,
I am an agent
of the powerful Six Companies,
and I herewith order you
to pay this Chinaman

for his washing,
and this Chinaman
for his services.

And mark you,
if you don't,
your life
won't be safe a minute.

DORA What shall I do?
What shall I do?

SLIM CHUNK PIN Go and sell your gold watch
and chain.

We will wait here
till you return.

Go!

DORA Oh, heavens!
Oh, heavens!

Dora exits.

AH COY White people damn fools.
Too muchee eaty,
too muchee drinkee.

SLIM CHUNK PIN Dry up, will you?

(Slaps Ah Coy)

You are too muchee smart,
too muchee sassy.

This is the sixth time
in eight months
we have furnished you

with a situation, and now
you are on our hands again.
If we had all such chickens
as you,
the importation of coolies
would be a bad speculation.

You have not half paid
your passage money yet.

AH COY   Me like heep work.

SLIM CHUNK PIN   Shut up, you rat-smasher!

(*Slaps Ah Coy*)

Mind, now,
if you don't improve
you will get your wind cut off
one of these days.

We didn't import you
to lose money;
we can have that easier
by gambling in stocks.

(*To Ah Coy*)

Look at Sam.

He fulfills his contracts
with the company like a man,
and saves money besides.

AH COY   Sam Gin been here many years;
white people plenty money then.

White people no money now.
Chinaman take too muchee money to China.

Slim Chunk Pin slaps Ah Coy

SLIM CHUNK PIN   Stuff and nonsense;
what do you know about it?

Don't the mines
produce as well as ever?
We can do without
the white people altogether.
Why should we allow them
always to skim the cream
from the milk?
We have submitted to it
long enough!

In ten years more,
California will be ours!

Sam Gin!

Sam Gin kneels.

SAM GIN   Master.

SLIM CHUNK PIN   How much money have you saved?

SAM GIN   Three hundred dollars.

SLIM CHUNK PIN   Wouldn't you like to have
a washhouse for yourself?

You know
I am the man who has a say
about that.

SAM GIN   I much likee washhouse.

SLIM CHUNK PIN   All right,
you shall have one.

AH COY Too muchee washhouse no good;
me no make money.

SLIM CHUNK PIN Because you trust a crowd
like these people here,
you fool.

(*Slaps Ah Coy*)

Sam,
if you start a washhouse
you will need
a nice-looking China girl.
White people like to see them—
sabee?

SAM GIN How muchee two?

SLIM CHUNK PIN One is enough for the
present.

SAM GIN How muchee one?

SLIM CHUNK PIN The price depends on her age.
How old do you want her to be?

SAM GIN Twelve years.

SLIM CHUNK PIN Look,
that old rascal!
He likes something tender.

Well,
I sell you a nice-looking girl
for two hundred dollars,
cash on delivery.

SAM GIN Two hundred dollars,
too muchee money.

SLIM CHUNK PIN   That is cheap, Sam,
depend on it.

Some years ago,
we used to get one thousand
dollars for a good-looking Chinese
girl.

SAM GIN   I take one.

SLIM CHUNK PIN   All right,
I will pick you out a
good one.

But you must know, Sam,
that I always pack my girl
in a box when I deliver them,
to prevent other Chinaman
from running away with them,
sabee?

SAM GIN   I sabee!

SLIM CHUNK PIN   When I send the box
you must have the coin on hand—
sabee?

SAM GIN   Me catchee the money.

SLIM CHUNK PIN   Well,
it takes that woman a long time
to sell her watch.

Somebody is coming.

Frank enters.

FRANK   Stuck again.
Lost every cent;

Jack Flint, you are too sharp for me.

Frank looks up and sees the Chinese.

Hallo!
What do you want?

SLIM CHUNK PIN I am an agent
for the powerful Six Companies,
and am ordered to see
Chinamen are paid.

FRANK Get out of here,
powerful quick,
you slave dealer!

SLIM CHUNK PIN I won't!

FRANK Take that with you!

Frank strikes the Chinese and kicks them out.

Frank to the audience.

FRANK That's the way to make them go!

G.

Visa and CHINAMAN *sit on two separate sides of the stage.*

Visa lip-synchs the following. Visa's dialogue is spoken by a company member using the offstage mike.

SLIDE: BLUE

VISA Blue

CHINAMAN Blue

VISA That's what I remember most
about the crossing

CHINAMAN That's what I remember most
about the crossing

VISA Blue

CHINAMAN Blue

VISA A lush expanse of placid blue

CHINAMAN A torrential roar of ocean blue

VISA Blue of a TV screen

CHINAMAN Blue of an autumn moon

VISA Suddenly
an occasional island of

SLIDE: WHITE

CHINAMAN A cloud above
lone dancing

VISA An unexpected adornment
A sigh
A slight reprieve

CHINAMAN Or
a burst of a failing sun
on turbulent waters
a shimmering carpet of gold and

SLIDE: RED

VISA Then
as abruptly as they appear

CHINAMAN   They disappear

VISA   A return to

CHINAMAN   Back to

SLIDE: BLUE

VISA   Sky blue

CHINAMAN   Ocean blue

VISA   Endless blue

CHINAMAN   Blue

VISA   Blue

CHINAMAN   I see
this blue
through this porthole
of a wooden slipper
I capture
the salty topaz
in my lungs

VISA   Through the porthole
this small window of the metallic bird
I capture
the sky
the containable
obtainable
blue

CHINAMAN   I capture the infinite possibilities
of the new world

VISA   Of *mei guo*

CHINAMAN Of beautiful country

VISA Of this place called America

CHINAMAN Through the porthole of the boat
this small window
I see
turbulent murky mysterious blue
I see
it claim limp bodies
of friends
family
dead from epidemic meningitis
The boat reeked their legacies
Waves of grime sweat vomit

VISA I close the vomit bag
giddy from turbulent skies
In my hand
a crumpled plane ticket
American Airlines

CHINAMAN A wrinkled paper in alien language
A sojourner's promise of work
Passage to mountains of gold

VISA In my Levi 501s
I stare
souvenirs of a home in past tense
coins
loose change

CHINAMAN Denominations of home
in pieces
like memory

VISA Instead
I look up
look toward
a land of

CHINAMAN The pursuit of

     SLIDE: LIBERTY

     SLIDE: HAPPINESS

     SLIDE: OPPORTUNITY

VISA A country bathed in a Hollywood halo

CHINAMAN A land
spoken in excited hush whispers
in town squares
family dinners
in Toisan
in China

VISA I have long lived in America
in its pages
glossy pages of

     SLIDE: *VOGUE*

     SLIDE: *PEOPLE*

     SLIDE *COSMOPOLITAN*

VISA I have long lived there
in the blue small windows of America
in its slices of lives
the lives of

     SLIDE: *FRIENDS*

SLIDE: *HAPPY DAYS*

SLIDE: *HOME IMPROVEMENT*

VISA These
the promises of a new life
in the new world

CHINAMAN I arrive finally
in heaven
where angels live
So appropriate
as they call this place
Angel Island

VISA From sky blue comes

SLIDE: WHITE

VISA Formica white
the counters of immigration

SLIDE: PASSPORT PLEASE!

CHINAMAN White
the faces of men I encounter

Visa and Chinaman face the screen.

SLIDE: WHY ARE YOU HERE?

SLIDE: BUSINESS OR PLEASURE?

SLIDE: HOW LONG WILL YOU
BE HERE FOR?

SLIDE: WHERE IS PENANG?

SLIDE: IS THAT IN JAPAN?

SLIDE: CHINA?

SLIDE: KOREA?

SLIDE: THAILAND?

SLIDE: PHILIPPINES?

Visa turns to the audience.

VISA   A verbal barrage begins
       A geography lesson
       where in Asia I'm from
       A history lesson
       what country I'm from
       A grilling
       An interrogation
       A torrent of words questions answers
       A flutter of visa papers
       landing cards
       A studied glance
       from the immigration officer
       A sudden reprieve
       A sapphire blue

       His eyes

       This officer
       A look of an angel
       A welcome mat to the country beautiful

Chinaman turns to the audience and sits on the chair.

CHINAMAN   A quarantine
           A barrack
           they put me in

           A fence
           they separate me from

A building
they confine me to

A cell
from which I can see
A city
named after a saint

San Francisco

A glimmering jewel
this city
a hope
a vision

VISA   After minutes

CHINAMAN   After days weeks months

VISA   Losing count

CHINAMAN   The immigration officer

VISA   With eyes blue
he smiles

CHINAMAN   He says
I can go

VISA   Says he wants to know
if I like
coffee

CHINAMAN   He says
to join the other Chinamen
over there

There!

There!

Move there!

VISA Says
he wants to have coffee with me

Says
Starbucks
West Hollywood
Eight o'clock

Says
it's his national duty to

SLIDE: WELCOME

VISA Welcome me
Says welcome
to the City of Angels

Welcome to Los Angeles

Chinaman walks downstage and steps on the fabric. He ends up across the stage from Visa.

CHINAMAN We march in a single line
with luggage and work papers
in hand
Our hats
in the other

VISA The immigration officer
George
His name is George
He waves

CHINAMAN Waves us over
Waves us outside

VISA Once outside
I look up

Visa and Chinaman look up.

CHINAMAN Into the sky

VISA I look out

Visa and Chinaman look out into the audience.

CHINAMAN I see the ocean

VISA It seems different
from this shore

CHINAMAN It seems the same
from this shore

Chinaman looks ambivalent.

VISA I know
I'm going to like it here

Visa smiles.

SLIDE: WELCOME TO AMERICA

Visa and Chinaman look at each other.

H.

Visa dances.

A zither, a Chinese string instrument, plays a traditional Chinese song on the side stage.

A Super-8 home movie is projected on the screen. The home movie is of a Caucasian-American family in a family activity, i.e. picnicking, birthday parties, swimming, etc.

As the dance ends, Visa walks downstage in front of the Super-8 projector. The film lands on Visa's abdomen. We see the film projected on his body. Visa caresses the image as he would a baby.

Visa runs off. The blurred projection jumps back onto the screen. It remains blurred.

I.

SLIDE: 1930s

SLIDE: ALASKA, SEATTLE, AND
         LOS ANGELES

SLIDE: THE DANCE OF
         FILIPINO MIGRANT
         WORKERS

On stage, the CHORUS sits on chairs and dances to the choreography.

WORKER   Slice head
             Cut tail
             Hack fins
             Gut guts
             Half a minute
             Alaskan salmon
             in a can

             Slice head
             Cut tail
             Hack fins

Gut guts
Half a minute
Seventeen hundred
salmon a day

Wash wash wash
the dead dead fish
Scale scale scale and clean
Quick sliver
gang knives
six blades
Cut cut
into around the fish
to size
tin cans
for general stores
fit for generals

In poor light
we seal steam test the cans

Watch the burn!

In poor light
we wash wash beheaded fish
Watch the lye!

In poor light
Luis he cuts the—
Luis!
Watch the—!
Watch out—!
Cutting machine!
Right arm—!
Right—!

Arm—!
You—!
Slash—!
It—!
Off—!

Quickly
like magic hands that cut salmon
Swiftly
in half a minute
you do not cry out
Luis
your arm
it floats
down water red
among salmon heads

Hey Bongbong
Don't gimme
Don't pass
Don't want no literature
Don't want no workers' utopia

Hey Nando
Stop telling us
Secret meetings
Union
Equality
Farm workers uniting
in these United States of America

Don't want no trouble
Don't want no problems
Just a little peace
Just a little paycheck

A little something for mama
in Luzon
A little something for me
in America

Look out
Nando Sammy Bongbong
while you are eating
in a restaurant cross town
labor contractors
their quick sliver
gang knives
six blades
find their home
in Nando's gut
Sammy's and Bongbong's too
Cut cut them to size
throw them into the ocean
fit for salmon

After season
after Alaska
Seattle

Max the foreman
he hands me
slip of paper
I look at mine
Yellow with lines numbers English
Neatly itemized
one two three
Expenditures
during the season
Expenditures
I incur

25
withdrawals
100
room and board
20
bedding
20 for something
After all the deductions
at bottom line
13
Lucky number
13
to buy me a piece of America
I look stare
at the number numb
as if a dream
Tell me there are zeroes missing
All I see
13
in my hand
crumpled paper
with zeroes missing

I do nothing
Can't
Can't
Can't go back
back to lonely hotel
hotel brimming with lonely men
Back to squalid room
Back to bed
where my suitcase toothbrush photos
they wait
wait

wait
and wait

Instead
I breeze
run
storm into the dry goods store
Jackson Street
Put on a pair of corduroys
Slip into luminous blue shirt
Slide out into wet rainy streets
feeling like a million bucks

My Pinoy brothers
cannery workers
out on streets Seattle
losing themselves
cards
chips
in crowded Chinese gambling houses
losing their season's earnings
losing themselves in whiskey bootleg

My Pinoy brothers
they turn quarrelsome
abusive to their own brothers
when hearts and spades
dwindle earnings to zero

When
cards of diamonds and clubs deny
their fishy-smelling hands
turn attention
turn to
the willing company

plump fleshy
scantily clad
smiling women

Smiling women
stop smiling
when temporary love
dwindle earnings to zero

Once again
Pinoys hurled back
wet pavements
hotel rooms
overlooking a city of lights
in deep recesses of night

Oh
lights
lights
dancing lights
laughing lights

A building
nondescript
neon ablaze
A welcome
Manila Dance Hall

(*Music begins*)

Brightly dressed
white women
Beautiful
like Rita Hayworth
with heels high
dresses white

smiles gay
Like swans
they lift their gowns diaphanous
they climb sturdy stairs

Doors opening
Room swimming
Orchestra playing
Hypnotic
Erotic
It calls to me
Hands in pocket
I enter

My Pinoy brothers
cannery workers
domestic servants
I follow them
Feel lonely for the sound of home

The dance hall
Our makeshift home away from home
Scant Garbos Turners Grables
they luminate

For a night
we are princes of the city
Suits snappy
Fingers snapping
Hair back
Hands cologned
Hands with tickets
Ten cents a ticket
Ten cents a dance
with Girl American

Surely
three minutes
dancing with dream American
is worth a life of
bedding Alaskan salmon

As music plays
our wages
earnings
evaporate
dwindle to zero
All spent
on dance floors
Every Ellington note
Every Sinatra bar
Dancing with dream American

As I
my tickets
sit exhausted
I see the swans
their consorts
dance in graceful
distant delight

In an ocean faraway
in an ocean of tickets torn
I wait
wait
wait
and wait

Far upstage, Visa lip-synchs to the following song.

On the side stage, a SINGER *sings a song into the mike.*

The ENTIRE CAST *dance in couples.*

SINGER   Leaving
Going
Moving
Waving
Holding
Crying
Missing
Sailing

Dancing
Dancing
Dancing
on ocean blue

Working
Toiling
Burning
Sweating
Pulling
Pushing
Cutting
Planting

Dancing
Dancing
Dancing
in the endless fields

(*Dancers leave the stage. The Worker sits alone in the sea of chairs. Worker listens to the song and mouths the last stanza of the song.*)

Dancing
Dancing
The thought of you
Dancing

Dancing
far away

Longing
Loving
Holding
Waiting
Yearning
Dreaming
Sighing
Wishing

Coming
Coming
Wish I was coming
home

Dancing
Dancing
on dance floor

Dancing
Dancing
Ten cents a dancing

Dancing
Dancing
to forget you
I'm not
coming

Baby
I'm not
coming home

Dancing
Dancing

Dancing
alone

Worker is alone on stage.

J.

SLIDE: TESTIMONY

SLIDE: JOSE CASAS

JOSE CASAS *is Mexican-American.*

JOSE   Look at me.
How many of you would think Chinese?
I am,
a little bit, that is.
My grandfather,
he was Mexicano

But he was also Chinese.
He was,
as our family would say,
our Chinese *abuelito.*
Our Chinese grandpa.
His name was Marty Le Wong.
It's true.

My great-grandfather left China
at the turn of century
with his family
because he was afraid
of getting caught in the Boxer Rebellion.

After a few years,
my grandfather's family found a home

for themselves
in Mexico,
of all places.

He would come to California
every few years for visits,
and I still remember
the last time he came to Los Angeles.

I was about eleven or twelve at the time,
and towards the end of this particular visit
my mother's *compadre* suggested
that he take me to Chinatown,
which was really good for my mom
because he didn't even know
there was a Chinatown in L.A.

It was nice
having my grandfather around.
He was different.

I can still picture it
like it was yesterday,
my *abuelito* falling in love
with Chinatown.

You have to remember,
he was from Mexico
where there weren't too many Chinese.

He stuffed himself
with as much damn Chinese food
as possible.

But
if there's anything I remember

it's the conversations
my grandfather would strike up
with just about anyone who would listen.

The people in Chinatown
were surprised to hear my *abuelito*
talking to them in their own language.

I mean,
they know he had some Chinese in him,
but since
he was also a Mexicano,
he stood out.

Funny thing is
not one person in Chinatown
even knew that Chinese
live in the heart of central Mexico.

My grandfather,
he passed away since that visit,
and I still think about that day
in Chinatown
every now and then.

And if anything,
it reminds me
that I often take things for granted.

I miss him.
He was always trying to teach me
about what it meant to be Chinese,
and I never listened.

And now
I wish I had.

Being right here,
right now
in Chinatown,
how could I not?

I want to trace my Asian heritage,
maybe even go to China one day.

I think
my Chinese *abuelito*
would have loved that.

K.

Forties music swells up and plays.

SLIDE: World War II

SLIDE: 9,400 Japanese
Americans in Los
Angeles were
unjustly expelled
from their homes.

SLIDE: These internees
spent several
months in temporary
assembly centers.

SLIDE: The temporary
assembly centers
were created
out of converted
stables at the
Santa Anita
and Tanforan racetracks.

SLIDE: Internees were then
           herded off in buses
           and trains

SLIDE: to a concentration
           camp in Manzanar,
           California.

L.

SLIDE: HOW TO TELL YOUR
           FRIENDS FROM THE
           JAPS

SLIDE: DECEMBER 22, 1941

SLIDE: *TIME*

Breezy forties music plays.

A fashion runway. A very camp Truman Capote–esque MC takes to the mike.

MC   It's 1941
      Can you tell your friends from the Japs?
      Here are some helpful tips
      to tell
      the friend from the enemy

(*A* JAPANESE MODEL *wearing horn-rimmed glasses and a* CHINESE MODEL *enter.*)

MC   Some Chinese are tall
      Virtually
      all Japanese are short

      Japanese are stockier and more broad-hipped
      than the Chinese

Japanese are seldom fat
They often dry up and grow lean
as they age

The Chinese often put on weight
particularly if they are prosperous

Chinese are not as hairy as Japanese

Most Chinese avoid horn-rimmed spectacles

Although both the Japanese and Chinese
have the typical epicanthic fold
of the upper eyelid
(which makes them look almond-eyed)
Japanese eyes are closer together

The Chinese expression
is likely to be more placid
kindly
open
The Japanese expression
is more positive
dogmatic
arrogant

Japanese are hesitant
nervous in conversation
laugh loudly at the wrong time

Japanese walk stiffly erect
hard-heeled
Chinese walk more relaxedly
have an easy gait
they sometimes shuffle

See?

Japanese

Chinese

Japanese

Chinese

Can you tell the difference?

M.

SLIDE: RALPH LAZO WAS THE
ONLY MEXICAN
AMERICAN INTERNED
DURING WORLD WAR II.

SLIDE: RALPH WILLINGLY
FOLLOWED HIS
JAPANESE FRIENDS TO
THE INTERNMENT CAMPS.

YOSHI *is playing baseball with* RALPH LAZO. *Ralph is miming the use of a bat. Yoshi mimes the pitching of the ball.*

Yoshi and Ralph face the audience. They never look at each other and play the scene naturalistically.

Yoshi throws the ball at Ralph. Ralph misses.

YOSHI Hey spud
You bat like a girl!

Yoshi throws the ball at Ralph. Ralph misses.

RALPH Damn!

YOSHI Swear word
You're going to hell!

218

RALPH Shut up and gimme the ball!

Yoshi throws the ball at Ralph. Ralph misses.

YOSHI That was an easy one, spud
You wanna try another game
Like Monopoly or something?

RALPH I'll get it right

Yoshi throws the ball at Ralph. Ralph misses.

YOSHI Hey spud
Been meaning to ask
Why are you here?

I mean
you didn't have to come
The Mexicans they didn't have to come
Didn't

But you did

I didn't want to come here
but I had to
My family
they had to

But you
you had a choice

You trying to be a hero or something, spud?

RALPH No
Just wanna be here

Okay with you?

YOSHI Hey
It's okay with me

RALPH Okay then

Yoshi throws the ball at Ralph. Ralph misses.

YOSHI Don't you miss your dad or something, spud?

RALPH No, not really
He's never around

YOSHI I know that
Is that why you're here?

RALPH Maybe
He's never around because—
because he's an artist

YOSHI An artist?

RALPH A housepainter
And sometimes he's a muralist

YOSHI Isn't that the same thing?

RALPH No
He gets paid to be a housepainter

YOSHI I knew that

RALPH Sure you did, spudhead

Yoshi throws the ball at Ralph. Ralph misses.

RALPH He's clueless

YOSHI Who?

RALPH My dad
You wouldn't believe

what I told him to get here
I told him I was going to camp

YOSHI He let you come here?

RALPH Well
I said
I was going to a Boy Scout–type camp

Yoshi and Ralph laugh.

YOSHI Wicked

RALPH Wicked

Yoshi throws the ball at Ralph. Ralph misses.

YOSHI My dad
he hardly talks anymore
since the evacuation
He's got this blank look on his face

RALPH Yeah I know

YOSHI He just sits there at the dinner table
Playing with his food
Nothing to say
Stares at Mum and me
Then as if he's embarrassed or something
he looks away
Looks out through the barrack windows
Stares at the barbed wire fence

RALPH There was one time
I saw him
standing by the fence
looking at it for a long time
Then he began to grab it

the fence
Then he rattled it
fiercely
like some animal that wanted to get out

YOSHI   He's never around anymore
I miss him

Yoshi throws the ball at Ralph. Ralph misses.

RALPH   You miss Belmont High?

YOSHI   Sorta

RALPH   The neighborhood?

YOSHI   Yeah kinda

RALPH   I almost don't remember
what Bunker Hill looks like

YOSHI   Sure you do
You remember Temple Street
You remember my house

RALPH   Of course
I ate there all the time

YOSHI   Baseball
at the Filipino Community Church

RALPH   Confession!

YOSHI   What?

RALPH   I joined the church
so I could play baseball

YOSHI   You're going to hell!

Yoshi and Ralph laugh.

Yoshi throws the ball at Ralph. Ralph misses.

YOSHI   The old neighborhood

Now we only have this
Dust
Mountains in the distance
Manzanar

RALPH   Seems we spend most days
playing baseball
I'm sick of *playing* baseball

And one day
we'll miss playing baseball
in Manzanar

Yoshi throws the ball at Ralph. Ralph misses.

YOSHI   Can I ask you another question?

RALPH   Jesus, Yoshi
you're full of frigging questions today
Let's play ball

YOSHI   Do you think I'm the enemy?
The Jap enemy?

Yoshi throws the ball at Ralph. Ralph misses.

RALPH   Heck no
You're not the enemy

YOSHI   How come you're so sure?
I mean
I could be some kamikaze spy
Spying for Japan or something

RALPH   'Cause the Japs are not that stupid, spud
            They'll choose someone else
            Someone with brains

Yoshi throws the ball at Ralph. Ralph misses.

YOSHI   Do you ever think about it, though?

            Maybe some of us are really
            working for Japan
            Undercover spies or something
            Planning some big plan
            to invade the United States
            Maybe they were right
            to put us in here
            just in case—
            so that—
            like insurance or something
            that something wouldn't happen,
            you know?

Yoshi throws the ball at Ralph. Ralph misses.

RALPH   Can I ask you a question?

YOSHI   Fire, spud

RALPH   If the Japs came over here
            To California, I mean
            I've been reading about
            bomb balloons they've been sending
            flying from Japan to America
            exploding
            killing Americans and stuff

            I mean
            if the Japs came over here

will you be on our side
or their side?

YOSHI   What do you think, spudhead?

RALPH   Don't know
That's why I'm asking you

Yoshi throws the ball at Ralph. Ralph misses.

RALPH   Wouldn't it be weird
to kill someone who looks like you?

I mean
it's easier to kill someone
who looks like somebody else
don't you think?

Yoshi walks downstage and looks at Ralph. Ralph turns to Yoshi.
This is the first time they look at each other.

YOSHI   Ralph
I wouldn't kill you

RALPH   I knew that, Yoshi

Ralph and Yoshi turn away from each other.

YOSHI   Spud

RALPH   Spud

Yoshi throws the ball at Ralph. Ralph misses.

SLIDE: RALPH LAZO DIED IN
LOS ANGELES IN
1992.

N.

SLIDE: A STORY OF TWO
        MOTHERS

SLIDE: ON TWO SIDES OF THE
        OCEAN

On one side of the stage, MOTHER *and Visa sitting side-by-side.
They look at an English phrase book.*

On the other, MARY *is putting on makeup, ready for an evening on
the town.* AH MA *looks at Mary from a distance.*

VISA Yes

MOTHER Yes

VISA Yes

MOTHER Yes

VISA No

MOTHER No

VISA No

MOTHER No

VISA Yes no

MOTHER Yes no

VISA Yes

MOTHER No

VISA Yes

MOTHER No

VISA No

MOTHER Yes

VISA Yes

MOTHER No

VISA Yes

MOTHER Yes

VISA Yes

MOTHER Yes

In another corner of the stage.

MARY Ah ma
I'm going out

AH MA Ah Mei

MARY Mary

AH MA Ah Mei

MARY Mary
Mary
Mary
Ah ma

AH MA Ma-lee
Ma-lee
Ma hai cue lay lore
Ma hai yacht yong
(That's what I said
Isn't it the same?)
Ah Mei
Ma-lee
Ah Mei

MARY Mary
   Hmm hei Ma-lee
   (Not Ma-lee)

   Ma–ree
   Christian name
   American name

AH MA Ah Mei
   lei kum marn cho ti fun lei
   (Come back early tonight)

MARY Huh?

AH MA *Cho ti fun lei*
   cho ti fun lei
   (Come back early tonight,
   Come back early tonight)

MARY What?

AH MA Early
   early come back

MARY Okay

AH MA Okay okay
   Everything okay

Pause.

AH MA *Lei sek bow mei ah*
   (Have you eaten?)

MARY *Sek bow sigh*
   Sek bow sigh
   (I have eaten already)

     Full
     Ate at McDonald's already

AH MA Ha?
     (What?)

MARY Nothing

In another corner of the stage.

VISA How are your hands?

MOTHER Good

VISA Painful?

MOTHER No

VISA You are in pain

MOTHER It's nothing
     Just a little
     A little here
     A little there
     I have some ointment
     White flower

     Let me make you some dinner

VISA I ate already

MOTHER McDonald's?

VISA Yes

MOTHER Are you going to work?

VISA Yes.

MOTHER Who will you be tonight?

VISA Tina Turner

MOTHER Classy
"Proud Mary"

VISA Right.
You want to come?

MOTHER I'm too tired

VISA Come

MOTHER I don't know
I have so much to do

VISA Come
Come
Come to the club

MOTHER I work ten hour a day
Come home
Make dinner
Clean house

Silence.

VISA You are embarrassed
by me

MOTHER I have to clean house

Beat.

VISA Okay
You have to clean house

In another corner of the stage.

AH MA Ah Mei

MARY Yes

AH MA You
My number one

MARY *Dai yet core* (number one)

AH MA Hmm
Dai yet core (number one)
girl
door-ter

MARY *Dai yet core leu*
(number one daughter)

AH MA *Ngnor how teoi hmm chee*
(I am very sorry)
Mm sek kong eng mun
(Don't know how to speak English)
Chang hei sek kong kong tung war
(Only know how to speak Cantonese)
How tor yeah shiong kong bei
lei tang
(So much to say to you)

Ah Ma lovingly holds Mary's face.

AH MA *xiong kong ngor ow lei*
(Want to say I love you)
xiong kong lei ker chin toe
ho chung yew
(Want to say your future is
very important)
xiong kong
(Want to say)
xiong kong ho door yeah
(Want to say so much)
putt kor ngor mm sek kong

                    (But I don't know how to say)
                    lei yeow mm sek tang
                    mm sek tang
                    (And you don't know
                    understand)
                    ngor yeow mm sek kong
                    mm sek kong
                    (And I don't how to say,
                    don't know how to say)

Pause.

MARY Ah ma
         Don't understand
         Don't understand

AH MA No?

MARY No

Mary touches Ah Ma's hands and leaves.

Ah Ma sits alone until the scene ends.

In another corner of the stage.

Visa helping Mother to put on makeup. Mother tries a shade of foundation.

VISA No

MOTHER Yes

VISA No

MOTHER Yes

VISA No

MOTHER Yes

VISA No

Visa points to the mirror.

MOTHER No

VISA No

Mother and Visa laugh. Mother tries another shade of foundation.

MOTHER Yes?

VISA No

Mother looks at mirror.

MOTHER No

Mary comes into Visa/Mother space and looks into the same mirror.

Visa puts some makeup on Mother.

VISA Yes

MOTHER Yes

VISA Yes

MOTHER Yes

VISA Yes

MARY Yes

MOTHER Yes yes yes

Mother then gets up and looks at the video screen and sings a song about homesickness and a mother's love as Visa looks on.

Mother then walks to the video screen looking longingly at the video. She stands in front of the video screen. Then Mother slowly caresses the screen.

O.

Visa looks at the FAN DANCER.

Fan Dancer dances.

SLIDE: 1959

SLIDE: Hiram Fong was the first American of Asian descent to be elected to the U.S. Senate when he was chosen as Hawaii's first senator.

SLIDE: 1962

SLIDE: Wing Luke was the first Asian American elected to public office anywhere in the continental United States when he won his Seattle City Council seat.

SLIDE: In 1966, March Fong Eu became the first Asian American

assemblywoman in
California

SLIDE: Eu was also
California's first
female secretary of
state for five
terms

SLIDE: until she was
appointed
ambassador to
Micronesia by
President Clinton

SLIDE: In 1996, Gary Locke
became the first
Asian American
state governor in
the continental
United States.

SLIDE: 1998

SLIDE: There are more than
fifty elected Asian
American state and
city officials

SLIDE: and more than one hundred
Asian American
judicial officals
in the state of
California.

P.

Percussive bamboo music.

BOAT PEOPLE *lie on stools facedown and simulate swimming.*

Chorus hold two or three reams of silk to simulate waves.

Boat People swim against rough currents.

Sea currents get rougher.

Boat People begin to drown.

After fighting with the rough seas, they drown.

Boat People, belly up, surface above the waves.

REFUGEE 1975
Bim Nguyen
soldier for twenty years
fled Vietnam
with his wife
his four sons
his two daughters

With fifty-one other refugees
on a small fishing boat
they escaped

Flash forward
1991
Sacramento
California

The Nguyens stayed home
watched TV
With thousands of other viewers
they saw

their children
flash on TV

Their three sons
and a young man named Tran
had stormed into
a Good Guys electronics store
taking forty-one hostages
terrorizing them

The Nguyens rushed to the scene
They tried to talk to the boys
but police said
their children
would not talk to them

"If they had let me
talk to my son
Pham
I could have talked him
out of it
to lay down their weapons"
their mother said
through an interpreter

Good boys
The boys attended Mass
every Sunday
One is an altar boy

Good boys

They helped around the house

Good boys

That very morning
they asked their father

permission
to go fishing

Good boys

They allowed two groups of hostages
to leave
Women and children
They tied the remaining hostages
with speaker wire
forced them to crawl
and kneel like dogs

Pointed their weapons
at hostages' head
Swore that they were about to fire

They even proposed a game
dividing the hostages
into two groups
flipping a coin to decide
which group gets shot first

"Let's shoot
at one of his legs first
to show that we mean business"

One Nguyen boy shot a man
in the thigh

At nightfall
a seventy-four-year-old man
had a diabetic seizure
One gunman shot him in the leg
warned him
the next time
he would shoot him in the head

A pregnant woman
suffered a miscarriage

The gunmen asked for
forty 1,000-year-old ginseng roots
four *Robocop* protective suits
bulletproof vests
one million dollars
a helicopter
capable of carrying forty people
a .45 caliber pistol
plane tickets to Thailand
to fight the Vietcong

When their picture appeared
on the closed circuit TV
one shouted
"Look!
We are going to be movie stars!"

Eight hours later
just as they began to fire
on the hostages
a swat team shot
killed two of the Nguyen children
seriously wounding the third

In their rampage
the boys have already killed
two store employees
and a customer

It is discovered
that the Nguyen boys
belong to the notorious gang
Oriental Boyz

MAN *sits on the floor downstage right. He pulls paper boats from a gunnysack and places them on the stage; he continues to do so until the end of the scene.*

GIRL *sits upstage center.* WOMAN *sits far stage left.*

A TAI CHI DANCER *dances alone and in silence in far upstage.*

MAN In Laos
mountain country
we grew corn and rice for food
poppies as cash crop
We farm an area for two three seasons
and we move to another area
after the soil has been exhausted

Here in America
you have
chemical fertilizers
pesticides

My people cannot read English
Cannot follow instructions
on pesticide packages
Many get sick from the spray
We don't understand
how to irrigate fields

WOMAN Everything we had
we left behind
What we had was good

Now
I am afraid we will leave behind
our history

our customs
our traditions   .

There are other people
people who are more clever than us
If they have something important
to remember
they simply write it on paper
We Hmong
have no writing
Whatever we want to remember
to keep
we must say as I am telling you now

(*Angry*)

We have no other skills
but farming
except we are not even farmers anymore

We are just unemployed soldiers
but the American government
has an obligation to us

We fought for twenty years
side by side
with the CIA in the "secret war"

My brother was killed
by North Vietnamese soldiers

I remember
the promise the CIA made to us
"You help us fight for your country
and if you can't win
we will take you with us
and we will help you"

They brought us here to America
but making a living here
has been extremely difficult for us

The Americans came to my country
and built the war there

Now
I have no country
I have nothing

Girl stands up reading an essay.

GIRL   Employment is a desperate problem
for the Mien and Hmong
Some try to make ends meet
selling handicrafts
like needlework
silver bracelets
and earrings
and by doing housecleaning
yard work

Most do not have jobs
Their unemployment rate
reaches as high as 90 percent

The Hmong constitute
what is becoming a welfare class

Most Hmong are barely surviving

MAN   Sometimes
sometimes I wake up
with nightmares
sometimes
three nights a week

My wife
she says
I am asleep
but she hears me screaming
"Get out! Get out!
The Communists are coming!"

I see my brother who they killed
I dream about him trying to find us
I dream they keep shooting him
and shooting him
until I wake up

GIRL   Seemingly healthy Hmong men
have died suddenly and mysteriously

Their deaths are medically unexplainable
and called the
"Hmong Sudden Death Syndrome"

Over one hundred have died so far
by the sudden death

They are generally men
about thirty to fifty years old
They have been soldiers for
fifteen to twenty years

They don't know
How to start life over again

They don't know how to farm
or work in a factory

WOMAN   If no one talks about our history
our traditions
they will disappear

We have lost our country
we have lost our fields
I am afraid our way of life is over

Whether it is good or bad
no one will know

Now we live in America
and we don't speak their language

Sometimes I feel invisible

GIRL   In one case

Girl looks at Man.

GIRL   A healthy man
age forty-eight
died from Sudden Death Syndrome

Girl looks at Woman.

GIRL   His wife had gone to an
English as Second Language class
that night

When she came home
she found the man depressed

Girl looks at Man.

GIRL   He said he felt lonely and missed home

They went to bed
and around 3 A.M.
she woke up.

The man was making a choking noise
and then died

Hmong also suffer from "survivor guilt"
Said one
"Why should I live
while others died at war?"

Said another
"I shouldn't be alive
while better men than me
like my elder brother
are dead"

Any questions?

Girl sits down.

WOMAN   I'm positive
we will lose our traditional religion
within the next ten years

There will be no more shamans
There will be no more scroll
There will be no more god

Maybe it's for the best
Maybe this is progress

Woman leaves Girl.

GIRL   Laos is like a dream

I escaped when I was eight
1976
Yeah
I can remember
pieces
bits and pieces
but that's all

MAN   Our village in Laos was ideal

The mountains for rice fields
were endless

There were big forests with game to hunt
Good streams
bamboo

GIRL   Right now
I'm in college
University of Wisconsin

Wisconsin
uhh
Can you just die?

I hope to graduate with a degree
in restaurant management

Yeah
I want to own a restaurant
in California someday

Yeah
I like California
There are more Asians there
And people don't look at you

Also
I feel much taller
in California

I've always felt
like an outsider here
here in Wisconsin

I feel more
more blended
in California
you know?

MAN   What I miss most from Laos
is my cow
I raised cows in the mountains

Sometimes
they would come from the jungle
and I would ride on the back of one cow

In Laos
we believed there were spirits
in the mountains

Here
Maybe the American Indians
believe in spirits

But those—

Man points to the mountains.

MAN   Those mountains
are *their* mountains
not ours

GIRL   I kinda see myself as a Hmong-American
and I'm making this country
America I mean

I'm making America my permanent home

What if
my parents want to go back to Laos?

Pause.

Girl looks at Man.

GIRL   They can go
But
I'm not going

No way

I'm staying

Staying

This is home
My home

Girl places a paper boat on the floor, and gets up and walks off stage.

MAN   My home

My home

Laos

Laos

I know I talk too much
dream too much
about Laos

But
this plant still has
some familiar soil
around its roots

Man places last paper boat on the floor.

MAN   I am learning to survive here
in America

Man gets up and joins Tai Chi Dancer in far upstage.

R.

JOSEPHINE *and* GERALDINE, *two Caucasian men in wigs, are women members of Friends of Asia. They have a Lady Bracknell quality about them.*

Josephine enters applauding.

JOSEPHINE   Wasn't that a lovely piece of
resistance on the little-known country
of Laos?
I went to Laos
on a holiday
when Bank of America sent my Chris
to head the Hong Kong office there
ten years ago.

Such tragic people
but
they have such great antiques.

I bought an ancient Buddha head
from Angkor Wat
With the help of Miss Martha Stewart,
I made it
into a most enchanting table lamp.

All of you must come to tea.

Look at these delightful little paper
boats
All handmade
Cute, aren't they?

Ah Ma,
please sweep them all away.

Mother enters with a broom and sweeps the paper boats away.

Come on.
Chop chop.

(*To Mother*)

You missed one.

So hard to find good help these days.

Now,
ladies and gentlemen,
we continue our Historical Heritage
Awareness Month Program
with something special.

Dear fellow Friends of Asia,
Geraldine and I
have been busy working
on this new modern dance interpretation
based on a true historical incident
that happened in Negro Alley,
just a few blocks south of here.

I'm sure
You'll find it most riveting.

Ladies and gentlemen,
without much further ado,
may I present
La Massacre du Chinois.

SLIDE: THE CHINESE MASSACRE

SLIDE: A REVISIT

Josephine and Geraldine dance to the music from the movie Titanic
*and do an Isodora Duncanesque dance of the Negro Alley Massacre
which is reminiscent of the hippos dancing ballet in Disney's* Fantasia.

S.

Visa dances on a lit blue square. Softly, Visa speaks the following monologue in Malay.

A company member stands at the microphone and recites the following monologue.

Above, a fluorescent light flickers on and off.

A soft zither accompaniment is heard.

VOICE   Room 543

    I sit
    in room 543
    where I bear witness
    a sea of men in towels white
    They migrate
    from room to endless room

    I lie
    anticipating on a narrow cot
    A small dimly lit room
    awaiting my history of moments
    in loose denominations
    of touches
    kisses
    sneers

    And I wait
    wait
    and wait

(Beat)

    Room 295

    While walking down Hope

251

near Grand
a man
homeless
street person
wearing army fatigues
a small dog
by his side
The man
he stares at me

He has a sign
cardboard brown
scrawled in blood red Crayola
"Vietnam vet
please help"
His trembling hand reaches out
in pouring punishing rain

Wordless
I ignore him
I walk by
walk around
walk away from him

He sees me
yells to me
"Gimme change!"
I say I have none
loose change

He says
"I fucking liberated your gook country
Gimme change"

I say
I'm from Malaysia
not Vietnam

He says
"All them gook countries
the same
you Vietcong
Vietminh?"

I say
I'm Malaysian

He says
"Makes no difference to me
Without us
you won't be in this country
won't be alive
Without us
you won't be walking down the street
in U.S. of fucking A
Gimme change"

He starts shouting
yelling
He says
"Isn't this rich?
the liberator is begging
for money
from gooks
I saved
From gooks
I killed
From gooks
I could have killed

Could have done you like My Lai
Isn't this rich?"

Embarrassed
Frantic
I dig deep into my 501s
Find round silver demoninations of
twenty-five
ten
five
Shower him with change
to buy his silence
The coins
they trickle onto his dusty palms

But they repel back
Back with force
Back with anger
Back to my face

"Keep your fucking change, gook
don't need it"

With that
head held high
the man walks away
and I quiet
at the corner
of Grand
and Hope

(*Beat*)

Room 897

I wonder
why my thoughts
in fragrant fluid Malay

sound different
from the brash nasal duck sounds
that is English
which emits
from my lips?

(*Beat*)

Room 521

I count the number of Georges in my life

George from immigration
George from Macy's
George from litigation
George from Guatemala
George from UCLA
HIV George on disability
George who-loved-and-knew-my-Asian-culture-
more-than-I-did-and-has-dated-the-entire-
Asian-population-in-L.A.
George Brown Smith Rosenblatt
George et cetera

A host of Georges
Georges of concrete jungles
Georges who never stayed long
Georges who don't return phone calls
Georges good for a moment
and
a moment is all I have

Surely
all these moments
these pieces
add up to something

(Beat)

Room 679

A partial list of things
that remind me of home:

The comfort of large trees
Gentle kisses on the neck
Rain
Schoolboys in uniforms
Noisy barbershops
A torrent of Cantonese
Sound of snipping scissors
Singing to Karen Carpenter
Upright piano with sheet music
McDonald's
Sighing in late afternoons
Spicy *mee goreng* noodles
Unruly unkempt bouganvillas
An unexpected smile from a child
Teaching my mama English from a phrase book
Madonna

(Beat)

Room 254

My mama
a petit woman
standing tall at five two
in Malayan Penang
smells of faint *blachan* and garlic
smiling
with two gold teeth
flashing
laughing

at the English words
I learned in primary school today
Yes no yes no
A refrain we repeated
we giggled
with glee
with delight
For hours
A simple conversation
she yes
I no
For hours
the two most important words
of the English language
Yes no

Mama
she always listened to scratchy 45s
twisting
rocking
rolling to
vinyl Elvis Presley
Al Martino
Tina Turner
if Mama wore a sequined skirt
if Mama wore spiked heels
if Mama came to the beautiful country
she would be Tina
instead of a pathetic old woman
scrubbing sweeping cleaning floors
of expatriates

Sometimes
late at night

I can still hear Mama
Her yes
I no
She no
my yes

(*Beat*)

Room 444

There is so much to live
to love
about this beautiful country

Every time
my feet finds this stage
Every time
the light drenches my skin
I am strangely home

My foundation
mascara
rouge
My new face
My lip-synch life
My makeover life in America

This theater
This is my home
My between home
between the port of Penang
and the port of Los Angeles
Forever
living in two worlds
Forever
belonging to none

I only wish
I wasn't lonely

(*Beat*)

Room 134

Here in room 134
I sit on
white Cloroxed sheets
waiting for a moment

Suddenly
this stranger
this George
he appears

Back lit
silent
wordless
touching
places familiar
saying
words familiar
with a smile familiar

And
I shut the door

Again

T.

SLIDE: THE BALLAD OF LILY
CHIN AND GUNNER
LINDBERG

SLIDE: A STORY OF TWO
KILLINGS

There are two chairs facing each other.

LILY *and* GUNNER *walk in straight lines on stage, never looking at each other.*

Lily sporadically calls out "Vincent" and "How come like that."

Gunner sporadically calls out "Dominic" and "Stop looking at me."

Lily and Gunner start running frantically and saying their lines urgently.

Suddenly, they stop.

LILY   My father he warn me
Life in America will be hard

But you marry Chinese-American
So you go with him

My husband
he serve U.S. Army in China
World War II

I get off boat
1948

We live and work in basement laundry
Highland Park high-class back then

When neighborhood kids see us
in basement
they make ugly face
stick out tongue
like this
and make like they cut out throat

GUNNER   Oh
                I killed a Jap a while ago

                I stabbed him to death
                at Tustin high school

                I walked up to him
                Dominic was with me
                and I seen this guy rollerblading

                And I had a knife

LILY   When I first come here
                I don't know anything

                So my husband
                he take me to new place
                go here, go there
                We go see baseball game
                but when people see
                Chinese people sit there
                they kick us
                curse us

                I never go back

GUNNER   We walk in the tennis court
                where he was
                I walked up to him
                Dominic was right there
                I walked right up to him
                and he was scared

                I looked at him and said
                "Oh, I thought I knew you"

And he got happy
that he wasn't gonna get jumped

Then I hit him

LILY That day
Vicki take Vincent to fix ring

When they buy ring
she skinny
Now
they have to make ring
bigger for wedding

Vincent get off work nine o'clock
That day he come home seven o'clock

I doing dishes
I ask him
why back so early?

He tell me he go out to bar
to club

I say
Vincent, don't come back too late
You getting married
Don't go to those places anymore
He say
Okay
Ma
this is last time

I say
Don't say "last time"
Very bad luck!

GUNNER I pulled the knife out
        a butcher knife
        and he said
        "no"

        Then I put the knife to his throat
        and asked him
        "Do you have a car?"

        And
        he grabbed my hand
        that I had the knife in
        and looked at me
        trying to get a description of me

        So I stomped on his head
        three times
        and each time said
        "stop looking at me"

        Then
        he was kinda knocked out
        dazed

LILY   In 1949

        I have operation
        and doctor say I cannot have baby

        But I love children
        so much
        I want to adopt

        I write home
        for picture from orphanage
        We like picture of four-year-old boy

He look so smart
It take over one year
to bring Vincent to Detroit

GUNNER   Then
         I stabbed him
         in the side
         about seven
         or eight times

         He rolled over a little
         So
         I stabbed his back about
         eighteen
         or nineteen times

LILY   I cry and cry
       Vicki she hold me

       I say
       over and over
       Vincent, Mama come
       You answer me
       Open your mouth
       Move your mouth
       Let Mama see you

       But no feeling

       I touch him
       so many time

GUNNER   Then he laid flat
         and I slit one side of his throat
         on his jugular vein

         Oh

The sounds
the guy was making were like
"Uhhh"

Then
Dominic said
"Do it again"
and I said
"I already did, dude"
"Ya, Do it again"

So
I cut his other jugular vein

LILY He tell me
Three year probation

He tell me
they only get $3,000 fine

I call Vincent boss right away
I say
Uncle Ping, how come like this?

He say
Nobody have courage to call me

I go to meeting
Everyone angry

But
they say
you cannot trial person second time
I say what trial?

All through court
no one talk to me
They just listen to defendent story

I say
it because those two are white

If they Chinese
it be different

I am mother!
Why don't they call me to go to court?

GUNNER   And
Dominic said
"Kill him, do it again"

I said
"He's already dead"

Dominic said
"Stab him in the heart"

So
I stabbed him
about
twenty
to twenty-one times
in the heart

LILY   I am grateful—

We all work hard—

I'm sorry I am not—

We all work very hard to get justice
for my son Vincent

GUNNER   Then
I wanted to go back and look
So we did

And he was dying
Just then
taking in some bloody gasps of air

So
I nudged his face
with my shoe
a few times

Then I told Dominic to kick him
So
he kicked the fuck out of his face

And
he still has blood over his shoes
all over

Then
I ditched the knife
after wiping it clean
onto the side of the I-5 freeway

LILY   I don't know what kind of law in America

We are all citizen
My husband
he stay in America fifty-seven year
He is American in American army

I don't know what kind of law in America
We pay tax the same
We only the skin type different

But heart
heart is same

GUNNER   Here's the clippings from the newspaper
and
we were on all the news channels

Gunner takes out his newspaper clipping and shows it to Lily.

Lily gets up from her chair and walks to Gunner. She takes out her photo of Vincent and shows it to Gunner. It should look like a Western gun standoff.

LILY   Please aaaa—

All of you—

Good and honest people—

Please—

Please—

I want everybody—
tell government—
do not drop this case—

I want justice
for Vincent—

I want justice
for my son—

Lily walks back to her chair. Gunner still holds out his newspaper clipping as if to give to Lily.

LILY   Thank you

Lily sits and looks at her photograph. Gunner sits reading his newspaper clipping.

SLIDE: VINCENT CHIN WAS
BEATEN TO DEATH
WITH A BASEBALL BAT

OUTSIDE MCDONALD'S
IN 1982.

SLIDE: LILY CHIN HAS SINCE
MOVED BACK TO
CHINA.

SLIDE: THIEN MINH LY WAS
FOUND STABBED TO
DEATH AT TUSTIN
HIGH SCHOOL TENNIS
COURTS.

SLIDE: IN A CALIFORNIA
COURT, GUNNER
LINDBERG WAS
SENTENCED TO DEATH
IN 1997.

U.

SLIDE: TESTIMONY

SLIDE: NANCY YEE

NANCY YEE *is an immigrant from Hong Kong.*

NANCY   About forty years ago
I from Hong Kong
Come to America
San Franisco

When the plane almost land
I look out the window
I see so many lights

269

The place so big
So beautiful

And I say to myself
"what a great place to start a new home"

I lived in Santa Cruz
about seventy miles from San Francisco

The town was really small
We only had two business
owned by Chinese
One is the restaurant
The other is the laundry

When I first come here
I don't know anything
I cannot read
write
talk
And of course
I cannot drive either
What can I do in here?

Later
I find a job in laundry
I work ten hour a day
I work very hard
But the hardest part is after work
I go home
I have no friend
Nobody to talk to
I am so lonely
All I do is cry and cry

Then
I'm thinking about what my mother say
She say
"No matter how far apart we are
we sleep under the same moon
every month
the full month night
you looking at the moon
and think about us
and we looking at the moon
and think about you
then our heart are together
and you will feel better"

Then
I thinking what my father say
He say
"You are *long how si*
You have to be careful
Think twice before you do anything
Think twice before you say anything
Do your best for everything
Then your dream will come true"

Thank you, Papa
I start learning English
I working very hard
I do the best for everything

After that
I'm smooth sailing

V.

MC   Ladies and gentlemen
It's my pleasure to bring back
Miss Visa Denied!

Visa comes out and lip-synchs and dances to Madonna's "Vogue."

SLIDE: 1998

SLIDE: Los Angeles

SLIDE: After my late shift
at Starbucks at
Pershing Square, I
walked along lonely
Los Angeles Street.

SLIDE: On the wet street
pavement I could
see a blue moon
dancing.

SLIDE: As if by command, I
ventured down the
same streets where
the Chinese lived
more than a hundred
years ago.

SLIDE: When I reached the
heart of the plaza,
I felt a stirring
of collective fear
the Chinese had.

SLIDE: In front, a city on
fire, eyes silent
with hate.

SLIDE: Behind, wagons,
          frenzied escape, a
          forced passage
          home.

SLIDE: It was more than a
          hundred years ago.

SLIDE: But the question is
          the still the same.

SLIDE: Stay or go?

SLIDE: Stay or go?

SLIDE: I'm staying.

SLIDE: I'm home.

*When Visa comes to the chorus of the song, the song skips repeatedly
for ten times. Visa is stunned and embarrassed by being on stage and
"voiceless." The music stops. Full fluorescent lights.*

MC Eh
        We have a technical difficulty.

Stagehands come to Visa with a bucket of water.

Visa looks at the two of them and nods. They help him undress.

Visa takes his wig and clothing off. He is naked.

Visa washes his face and wipes his face with a white towel.

Visa looks at the audience and speaks in broken and halting English.

VISA My
          name
          is
          Wong Kong Shin

I
come
from
Penang
West Malaysia

No

I
come
from
Los Angeles
California
United States of America

EPILOGUE

Visa walks to Immigration Officer facing us.

OFFICER   Passport please
Name?
Purpose of this trip
Purpose

Why are you here?
Business?
Pleasure?
Working?
Vacation?

I see

(*Visa holds out his hand.*)

Let me see your return ticket
Ticket

Plane ticket

Yes
that blue folder

No return
I see

You cannot stay
for more than three months

(Officer smiles at Visa. He stamps some papers and waves him over.)

Welcome to America

Next

THE END

WONDERLAND

Alec Mapa (Son), Joel de la Fuente (Young Man), Sab Shimono
(Man), and Tsai Chin (Woman)   Photo: Russell Caldwell

Wonderland was first presented in La Jolla on September 14, 1999, by the La Jolla Playhouse; Michael Grief, artistic director.

Young Man	Joel de la Fuente
Man	Sab Shimono
Woman	Tsai Chin
Son	Alec Mapa
Director	Lisa Peterson
Set Design	Rachel Hauck
Costume Design	Joyce Kim Lee
Lighting Design	Geoff Korf
Original Music and Sound Design	Mark Bennett
Dramaturge	Elizabeth Bennett
Production Stage Managers	Peter Van Dyke Tom Aberger

Wonderland is for Lisa Peterson.

WONDERLAND

A minimalist set.

The tone of the play is one of a nonmusical musical. Treat the monologues and dialogue as arias and duets.

Scene fluidity is key to this play.

Locations in the play should be indicated by lights and sound.

Props and set pieces should be employed at a minimum.

A YOUNG MAN, *dressed in a hip three-piece Armani suit, enters.*

YOUNG MAN   Sunrise

> In the far horizon
>> is a perfect sky
>> Cracked
> pried open
> by the piercing
>> rising sun

>> The sun's invisible golden rays
>>> shimmering
>>> glimmering
>> dancing
> on the restless sea

And above

(*Sound of roar of plane taking off*)

> Penetrating the hovering sky
>> a bird
>> silver
> slivering
>> winging
>> across Pacific waters

(MAN *is sitting.*)

We see a Man
             peering through
    a small porthole of the airplane
                    staring at the infinite blue sky
         wondering
if his ancestors
                 Chinese railroad workers
        made the very same journey
across the same ocean
                    almost two hundred years ago

MAN   I was in Singapore
          on business

          My company sent me there
          to assist the senior architects
          to supervise construction
          on a department store

          My company sent me there
          not because of the
          long hours
          long years
          I spent
          designing and drafting
          in architectural school

          My company sent me there
          because
          they thought
          as an Asian
          I'd have an upper hand
          in understanding

the social and cultural intricacies
of our Chinese clients

My company
assumed
I knew how to speak Chinese
presumed
I bowed the right way

Man smiles.

MAN   Thank God
the Chinese there
spoke fluent English
and they didn't even bow

YOUNG MAN   The year is 1965

And that
is my father
All of a strapping twenty-five
The dawn of his career
A man
brimming
grinning
with giddy excitement
ambition
and dreams

He arrives
in exotic tropical Singapore

There

Fragrant
frangipani flowers
wild orchids

                    bowing
            tipping
                    their flagrant heads
        to the occasional sigh of breeze

            Palm trees coconut trees ocean everywhere
                                        Paradise

(Sound of sixties rhumba music)

            It's evening
                            hot
                                balmy

                        We see
                            a beach
            an endless stretch of sandy white
            A quaint hotel
                        in the near distance

                    A building
            Victorian
                        white
                            colonial
            Glowing with light and laughter

                                The Raffles Hotel

(Young man assumes the role of a bartender and serves Man a drink.)

            And
                        there she is
        A woman of twenty-two
                Wrapped tight
        in a delicate silk *cheong sam*
                    Sipping a bright red umbrella drink
                        gin sling
                Sitting
                    at the Long Bar

    Sitting
        next to the Man in a three-piece suit

WOMAN Ay
    You tourist?
    No
    Then businessman
    I can tell

(*Man nods.*)

    Japan
    You come from Hong Kong
    Your English good
    So must not come from Asia, right?

(*Man shakes his head.*)

    You Australian
    No
    Not Australian
    You not very loud

(*Man laughs.*)

    Must be British
    No
    You not drunk enough

(*Man is about to answer.*)

    Don't tell me
    I'm good
    I can tell

(*Man whispers in woman's ear.*)

    Not American?
    American really
    Never meet Oriental from America before

So you what business?
What you do?

(Man speaks to woman.)

Wah
Architect
Sounds very important and exciting
Sorry but what is architect?

Of course
I just forgot
Too many gin slings

You design department store?
I love department store
I live in one
Almost
Actually I work in one
Salesgirl
Employee of the month
Twice
Really
You don't believe?

(Sound of Strauss' "Waltz of the Flowers")

Listen
A waltz
Strauss
I love

Let's dance
Come on

You American
and don't know how to dance?
Don't worry I teach

Ready?
You follow
I lead
Simple

Woman pulls Man's arm and leads him to dance.

YOUNG MAN   They dance
                    from the dance floor
                                to a room
                        at the Raffles

(*Sound of ocean roar*)

            Up above the hotel room

                Inside

                    A restless ceiling fan
                Endlessly groaning
            Listlessly moaning
                    Casting
                        flickering shuttered shadows
                            on moist
                                glistening bodies

        It's much later
                in the night

                    Shhh
                        Can you hear?

    A postcoital conversation is in progress
            The Woman
                    lying lazily beside the Man

The Man
        Doing what most men do best
            He's talking

                                    About himself

Man and woman lying in bed.

MAN   It's the latest thing in America—
        Started right in Texas—
        My company is constructing strip malls—

WOMAN   Strip—malls—?

MAN   Yes
        They are the new city centers
        The future town squares of America
        where people can come together
        commune socialize fraternize—

WOMAN   Really!—

MAN   These malls will dot all over America
        and no matter where you are from
        where you are
        when you come to a mall
        you'll feel right at home

        But
        I—
        I want—

WOMAN   What you want—?

MAN   Well
        I'm not going to design
        department stores forever
        This is only the first step
        of many steps

You see
I have
plans
dreams
big dreams
You may think this is silly
pompous even—

WOMAN   No—

MAN   I want to—
I'm going to revolutionize architecture

WOMAN   Really
You architecture revolutionary!

MAN   Yes
Architecture revolutionary!

Man and woman laugh.

Man gets up and unfolds his drawings. Drawings can be indicated by a box of light on the stage floor.

Man shows his drawings to Woman.

MAN   Look

WOMAN   This is so—

MAN   My drawings
They—

WOMAN   Beautiful
They are—

MAN   Thank you
You don't have to—

WOMAN   You very talented

MAN   I—
      I've never shown them to—

      I've been drawing
      in secret
      late at night
      for many years

      And one day
      one day these designs will be—
      I will—

      You see
      more than anything in the world
      more than life
      I want to birth
      tomorrow's concert halls
      cathedrals museums skyscrapers monuments

      My buildings will be unique
      bold
      gargantuan
      towering over cities and peoples
      reaching
      touching the heavens

      My buildings will stand tall
      forever and ever

      My contribution to history
      A part of history

Woman looks at Man admiringly.

WOMAN   Kiss me
         Kiss me

Man and Woman kiss.

YOUNG MAN   Four months fly by
               Four months of making love
       Four months of laughing
           dancing and gin slings
               Four months of being happy

    And
           at the end of four months
                 just when my father
        is to return to the States
            the following week—

WOMAN   I'm late—

MAN   Late?
    You mean—

WOMAN   Yes
    I'm pregnant
    I don't know what to—

MAN   Pregnant—

WOMAN   I don't usually—

MAN   It's all right—

WOMAN   I'm not that type of girl—

MAN   I know—

WOMAN   I was careful
    Careful not to—

MAN   I'll take care of it
    Let me think—

WOMAN   No
    I'll take care of it

Silence.

MAN What are you going to do—?

WOMAN I will go to doctor—

Man holds Woman's hands.

MAN This is all a part
of His design—

WOMAN Who's design?

MAN God's

WOMAN You Christian?

MAN Yes

WOMAN Oh god

MAN I love you

WOMAN Really?

MAN Really

WOMAN I love you too

MAN I feel so—

WOMAN Me too

Man and Woman kiss.

Man looks at Woman lovingly.

YOUNG MAN And my mother and father get married
with a minimum of fuss
A simple ceremony
in a little Methodist church
on a hill

Young Man assumes the role of a pastor.

WOMAN Wedding
      just like
      Elizabeth Taylor
      in *Father of the Bride*

Man and Woman standing side by side.

MAN She was radiant
     And I—
     I felt wonderful
     like I was standing
     on top of the world
     tiptoed
     I squeezed her petite hand
     and slipped a slim gold band on her finger

     This is the right thing to do
     It is
     It is

YOUNG MAN Again
          An airplane

           This time
             bound
    for the other side of the Pacific

(Sound of a plane taking off)

(Man sits with Woman, holding her hand.)

     The newlyweds
        sitting
      side by side

                    The Woman
              still clutching fast
                        her modest bouquet

                The Man
                        clutching fast
              his new drawings of buildings
                    yet to be built

                              Through the porthole
            she sees her homeland
                        growing smaller
                                    smaller
                                          in the distance

MAN   Happy?

WOMAN   Yes
            Very happy

Beat.

WOMAN   Chinese call America
            Mei Guo
            Beautiful Country
            Must be beautiful there
            Must be

            You know
            I always want to live in America
            I dream of going there since young

            First thing
            I will find job
            Working
            in big American department store
            Macy's

There
I hear they sell everything
Hangbag furniture moisturizer
I always want to work in Macy's
That is my dream

Oh
America
must be exactly like movies
Like *Sandpiper*
Did you see?
With Elizabeth Taylor?
Oh
I love Elizabeth Taylor!
In that movie
she live in beach house
near ocean
We must live near ocean
We must
We must
Just like *Sandpiper*

MAN (*Out*)   I thought for a moment
                     somewhat relieved
                     that she would blend in
                     very nicely in America

Sound of airport gate traffic.

YOUNG MAN   Los Angeles
                     in the golden state of California

Young man assumes the role of the immigration officer.

WOMAN   I arrive in America
                 in airport

White man
at immigration
He smile
he say
"Welcome to America"
He ask
Did I have a good flight?
He call me "honey"
I like

I say
"Yes
Very long journey
First time flying airplane"

He smile
Look at my passport
Eyes never at me
And he say
What I do
in Singapore for a living?
He call me "little lady"
I like

I say
"I work at Robinson's department store
Salesgirl
Twice employee of the month
I sell cosmetics
You must have heard
Max Factor?"

He smile
He say he know Max Factor
He call me "toots"

I don't know what "toots" mean
But I like

He say
How long I staying here
for vacation?

I say
"Oh, not here for vacation
Here forever"

He say
"What do you mean 'forever?'"

I show my finger
Small gold band
Twenty-four karats
I smile
I say
"I just got married"

This time
He doesn't smile
He mumble
"Congratulations"

I say
"I married American"

He say
"Do you have any papers?
Visa?
Immigration?
Marriage certificate?"

I say
"No

My husband
He has them"

The man frown at me
Motion to me
with his finger
"Wait a sec"
He don't call me "little lady honey toots"

He pick up a phone
Look at me
Say something
Look at me
Say something

All of a sudden
Two security guard
They come

The man at the counter
He smile
He say
I better follow them
They will ask more questions

I get worried
I say
"No
I really married
See?
Wedding ring?
See?

Let go
Let go!

Let me go!
Ouch!"

Just then
My husband
He walk straight to them
and say he has papers
But he has to stand in other line
Line for American only

The man
He smile again
This time
Half smile
Looking at marriage certificate
immigration papers
visa

He say
"Sorry
Procedure
Protocol
Just doing job
Welcome to America"

I say
"Thank you"
Then he say
to security guard
"Looks like they are bringing
more of their own kind in everyday"

My husband
He say nothing
Walk away

I don't think he hear
I don't think he want to hear

So I say
to smiling man
"Yes thank you
We bring more of our own kind in everyday
Toots"

I smile
I don't think
He like

Sound of traffic.

YOUNG MAN   Right in the heart of Hollywood

We're inside the love nest
small
cramped
untidy
modest
a typical bachelor apartment

Think William Holden's pad in *Sunset Boulevard*

You get the picture

Man ushers Woman in the apartment. Woman looks around the apartment.

Silence.

WOMAN   This is not *Sandpiper*
More like *Butterfield 8*

MAN   What?

WOMAN   Oh nothing
           Your place
           Very—
           Very—
           How to say?

MAN   Quaint?

WOMAN   Yes
           Quaint

YOUNG MAN   Things are not going well

WOMAN   Yes
           Very quaint

YOUNG MAN   Then she mounts her campaign
                        Operation Sandpiper

(*Sound of ocean*)

    Urging him to get a bigger place
                    for the two—
          the three—
             of them

(*Woman tugging Man's arm, pointing at various beach houses*)

      On weekends
             they drive to Santa Monica—

WOMAN (*To Man*)   *Sandpiper*—

YOUNG MAN   Spend afternoons in Venice Beach—

WOMAN   *Sandpiper*—

YOUNG MAN   Manhattan Beach—

WOMAN   *Sandpiper*—

YOUNG MAN   Redondo Beach—

WOMAN   *Sandpiper*—

YOUNG MAN   Laguna Beach—

WOMAN   *Sandpiper*—

YOUNG MAN   Any place
that has the word "beach" in its name—

WOMAN   *Sandpiper*—

YOUNG MAN   Any house with a beach in front of it

WOMAN   Isn't that house quaint?
Just like *Sandpiper*

Man looks at Woman. He nods. She smiles.

YOUNG MAN   Finally
she persuaded him to buy a house
on Malibu Beach
overlooking the ocean

WOMAN   It's so beautiful

MAN   Yes
A bit large for us I think

WOMAN   But look

House have wonderful view of sea
Sand everywhere
soft and fine like hair
Trees
with gray color bark

MAN   Eucalyptus

WOMAN   And look
pretty red butterfly
all flying about

What kind of butterfly?

MAN   Monarch

WOMAN   Monarch butterfly
Red butterfly

Red
very lucky color
See?
Good sign already

Inside house
we can put
a sofa
in front of wall
Red color sofa
And behind
Big painting
Oh
Teak coffee table
over there
and the whole house
all in baby blue

Very good feng shui—

MAN   It's beyond our price range
I don't think—

WOMAN   But you say
              you are architecture revolutionary right—?

MAN   I can't afford this on my—
          I'm only a junior in the company—

WOMAN   After you build more shopping mall
              sure you can afford—

MAN   Maybe we look at—
          There must be something else—

WOMAN   Once you become important architect
              have to entertain important client—

MAN   Something smaller—
          Something more—

WOMAN   And
              remember we need more room now
              especially for baby

Pause.

MAN   I guess
          I can take out a loan
          A mortgage
          Sign some papers and—

WOMAN   I love you

Man smiles at Woman.

MAN   What name are you going to give our house?

WOMAN   Oh
              that's easy

Woman smiles.

YOUNG MAN   Four months go by
                                                         at the Sandpiper
                                   the Man notices
                there is no discernible sign
                                                 of a swelling stomach

WOMAN   Don't worry
                            Sometimes tummy very small
                            Cannot see
                            But I feel him
                            I can
                            You want to
                            feel him?

MAN   How do you know
                   I mean
                   that it's a him
                   a son?

WOMAN   These things I know
                            I can feel
                            I know you also want
                            Right?
                            A son

MAN   Listen
                   The company finally gave me
                   my first assignment
                   my own assignment!

WOMAN   Monuments skyscrapers concert halls?

MAN   Well
                   not quite

                   I'll be designing
                   a strip mall
                   in downtown Camarillo

It's small
Nothing special
Nothing unique

But
all
on my own
all
of my own

And then
it's monuments—

WOMAN and **MAN**   Skyscrapers concert halls!

Man and Woman laugh.

MAN   So what did you do today?

WOMAN   Go out
look for job

MAN   And?

WOMAN   I go to Macy's
Big department store downtown

I tell them
I want to be Macy's salesgirl
Back in Singapore
I used to be salesgirl
Employee of the month

They smile
They say
things over here different
My experience in Singapore

five years
don't count

I say
"what difference?"
Still the same cosmetic
Same Max Factor
Same "Hello lady
nice color for lipstick
no?"

Right?

So
very quiet
they give me application

I try to fill up application
but don't understand application

So after one hour
I give them back application

But application all blank

They smile
They say
I cannot be effective Macy's salesgirl
I don't write English
Don't speak proper English
Maybe another time
Thank you
Good-bye

MAN   It'll come in time.

Beat.

WOMAN   Anyway
today I also learn from
TV cooking show
from Julia Child
how to make American food you like
Pork chops steak fries Lea and Perrin sauce
Tomorrow I make
Okay?

MAN   Okay

Man hugs Woman tightly.

YOUNG MAN   Aren't they just the cutest?

(*Sound of ocean*)

　　　　But
　　one day
after a long day
　　　　at the drafting table
　　　　　　　　at the construction site

　　The Man
　　　　he comes home—

WOMAN   I went to doctor today
And he say I'm not—

Not pregnant

I don't know what to say

I thought—
I thought I was pregnant

I was late
So I thought—

MAN   No, it's okay
       It's not your fault
       It's a mistake that anyone—

WOMAN   We can try again
         right?
         We can try—

MAN   Yes

Beat.

WOMAN   Maybe right now
         best you and me
         together alone
         spend time
         do husband and wife things together

         Ay
         I read in *Life* magazine
         about this place
         Cape Cod
         We go?
         Jackie Kennedy live there
         Cape Cod
         Sure to be fun

MAN   Yes, sure

       Didn't you go to a doctor in Singapore?

WOMAN   No—

MAN   Then how did you—

WOMAN   I miss period
         Vomit in morning so—
         So I thought—

MAN   I see

Man and Woman look at each other. Uncomfortable silence.

YOUNG MAN   Some time passes—

MAN   It's a good idea
you know
to have a little distance—

WOMAN   What you mean
"little distance?"—

MAN   A little distance
between us
A brief separation—

WOMAN   Why?—

MAN   Maybe you want to go back home
back to Singapore—

WOMAN   No—

MAN   I need some time alone—

WOMAN   For what?—

MAN   To think about things
about us—

WOMAN   Why?—

YOUNG MAN   And all of a sudden
Again

WOMAN (*Beaming*)   Guess what?
I'm pregnant

   Beat.

Man goes over to Woman and holds her.

Okay

So first time I say
I am pregnant
I lie
white lie

Don't get me wrong
I am not
like other sarong party girls
at Raffles Hotel
bat girly eyes
giggle giggle
hook white man
come to America
get Green Card
and then dump him

I love my husband
Really love him
And will try not to lie to him
again

But you know
sometimes men
they need extra help
Extra motivation
To make up mind

In the end
He happy
I happy

Happiness is everything

Sound of ocean.

SON *runs in.*

SON   Mom
        She loves telling me
            Her coming-to-America story
                Other kids get *Cinderella*
                Alice in Wonderland
                      And I get the "We-bring-more-
                      of-our-own-kind-in-everyday-
                      toots" for a bedtime story

      I'm sure it's real important
          But I never understand it
            She says—

WOMAN   Coming to this country
          A big sacrifice
          Don't forget
          You must be survivor
          Must be what again?

SON (*To Woman*)   Survivor

WOMAN   Yes
          Must be survivor
          Remember
          Must be success

SON (*To Woman*)   Must be success

WOMAN   Good

SON   But when I ask her
        more about where she's from
           She says—

WOMAN   So long ago
   So far away
   Better forget it
   Not important
   What is important is
   here and now
   You in America
   and success

SON   Maybe it's because they don't talk
   about stuff like that
    where she comes from

YOUNG MAN   That
      if you haven't been taking notes
      is me

       The Son
    And as you can tell
  from this very touching display of affection
   between mother and child
      we have a special bond
    and spend lots of quality time together

Sound of ocean.

SON   Can I go
   go outside and play?—

WOMAN   Only after you do it again—

SON   Mom!
   We did it fifteen gazillion times already!—

WOMAN   Don't you want to be
   successful?
   Have glamorous life?—

SON   One more time only
        And then I go—

WOMAN   Again
        From the top—

SON   Scene from *A Place in the Sun*
        With your favorite actress
          Elizabeth Taylor—

WOMAN   Right
        And where are we?—

SON   We're at the balcony
        And there's a party inside the house—

WOMAN   So who are you?—

SON   Montgomery Clift
        Before the car accident—

WOMAN   So still good-looking right?—

SON   Okay—

WOMAN   Ready?
        Action!

(*Sound of old movie music*)

        "And we'll have
        Such wonderful times together
        Just the two of us"

SON   "I'll be happiest person in the world"

WOMAN   "The second happiest"

SON   "If I can only tell you how much I love you
        If I can tell you all"

WOMAN   "Tell Mama
             Tell Mama"

             They kiss

Woman and Son kiss.

             Music
             Music
             Music

             Ahh
             So romantic

Sound of old movie music ends.

Son wipes his lips.

SON   Mom
                You are so weird

Woman and Son laugh. They hug each other.

Sound of ocean.

YOUNG MAN   Years dissolve
                     with a blink of the eye

                We are on the wood deck
                             of the Sandpiper
             with a view of the distant horizon
                         where the sky kisses the sea
                                 blue touching blue
                                         blue on blue

                 There
                     the Son sits
             with his school friend George
                 Two kids

                    the best of friends
                        the time of their lives

SON   George
            you know sometimes
                like late in the afternoons
                    after school
                        'stead of hanging with the gang
                            wandering aimlessly
                                in the mall or something

        I'd run
            here
                    straight here
                        flash
                            like the wind
                                right here
                                    And sit

        I'd look out
            into the sea
                and wait
                    wait
                        wait for that moment

        Then it appears
            clockwork
            Bam!

        You can always count on it
            It never lets you down
                It's there
                    Always there
                        Can you see it?

MAN (*To Son*) Can you see it?—

                        316

SON Can you?—

MAN Can you?—

SON There—

MAN There—

In this flashback sequence, Son acts as if he is ten years old.

SON (*To Man*) Yes—

MAN You're the only person I've ever shown it to
This is our special secret
See?—

SON Spectacular—

MAN The sun's reflection on ocean waters—

SON The sun's reflection on ocean waters—

MAN God's miracle—

SON A yellow brick road—

MAN On this sheet of ocean blue—

SON A hot blazing trail—

MAN Paved by dying sunlight—

SON Blinding light—

MAN Radiant light—

SON A magnificent golden carpet—

MAN Stretching stretching
straight into the horizon
far, far beyond—
Can you see it
can you?—

SON Wow!
    (Out) And sometimes
               sometimes I
                    I swear George
                         I hear it call out to me
                             Yeah
                                  Really—

MAN Come
    it says
    Come—

SON Come—

MAN This invisible voice tells me—

SON Leave everything behind—

MAN Escape—

SON Run to the great beyond
              But I always hesitate
                    Don't know why

  Like who the fuck is telling me shit like that?
              Certainly not—
                  No—
                        Not Him—
                            Not God—

MAN It's God's voice
    His voice
    "Whether you turn right or left
    you will hear a voice, saying
    'This is the path, walk on it'"
    Isaiah Thirty Twenty-One—

SON But at the same time—

MAN   Deep within me—

SON   Deep down—

MAN   A stirring—

SON   Fluttering—

MAN   A longing—

SON   An awake kinda feeling—

MAN   Telling me—

SON   Yeah
                    it can be true

      But
                    I hesitate
                    I wait
                              Maybe I'm chicken—

MAN   Then before I know it
      the sun winks its final wink—

SON   And the golden carpet—

MAN   Before my eyes—

SON   It crumbles
                disappears—

MAN   Dissolves into nothingness—

SON   But
                tomorrow—

MAN   I know it'll be there again
      The golden carpet
      God's gift—

Maybe I'm just talking nonsense—

SON (*To Man*)   No—

Man messes up Son's hair lovingly.

MAN   Maybe not—

Man leaves.

SON   George
                    You're the first person
                            I ever showed this to
                                    I know
                                            It's kinda stupid

                    Well
                            Forget it
                                    Forget what I said
                                            It's not important

                                                    It's not

Sound of office noise.

YOUNG MAN   Once again
                            years dissolve
                                    years fly by

(*Man mimes drawing at the drafting table.*)

                    1980
                The Man
                        He continues to build
                                    to father more strip malls
                                in sunny Southern California

320

All a little nondescript
                    All a little too many
               All a little too blah
                         You know the ones

          In the late of late nights
               We see him
     burning midnight oil
               toiling
          designing
                    drafting
                         shopping malls

Man stops drawing, looks at his designs, nods and smiles.

MAN   Yes
          Yes

Man mimes shaking hands with other people.

YOUNG MAN   1981

          We see the Man
                    shaking hands with contractors
               engineers
     business men in three-piece suits
                         at construction sites
                    cutting ribbons
                         completing yet another
               and another
                    and another
                         shopping mall

MAN   Thank you
          Thank you

Man mimes sketching, drawing, and tearing up papers.

YOUNG MAN   1982

And as soon as the ribbon is cut
the doors of the mall flung open
The Man finds himself
once again in the bowels
of his office
Designing drafting
Midwifing
Birthing
yet another shopping mall

But this time
It's a big one
It's—

Man stops working and looks up.

MAN   Wonderland

Sound of office noise.

YOUNG MAN   Downtown L.A.

In the crisscross grid of streets
Swirling in a cloud of
smog heat and dust
A silver building

In it
Peterson Peterson and Peterson
Dad's home away from home
His office
Fluorescent bright
The requisite Formica furniture
Drafting tables

Paper pencil erasers
                    litter the room

              It's morning—

Man runs on stage and stops.

MAN I run along the carpeted hallways
     burst into
     my colleagues' offices
     their cubicles
     carry a box of quality Cubans
     pop open bottles of sparkling champagne
     dole out cigars and plastic glasses
     to my surprised buddies pals and friends

Young Man assumes the role of Man's colleague.

Man gives Young Man a cigar.

     I tell them
     "Guess what?"
     with a smile on my face
     I say
     "It's done!
     It's finished!
     The Wonderland mall is completed!
     Took two years
     and it's finally done!"

     I did it

     A beautiful mall
     borne of the finest materials
     marble teak wood titanium
     Covered by a roof of metal and glass
     an arching butterfly's wing
     spanning the God-fearing skies

My creation
My latter-day Tower of Babel
touching
kissing the heavens

My first success of many successes
I built the largest shopping mall
in Southern California!
Right smack
along the shores of Santa Monica!

Over two hundred stores!
In this mall!

My mall

(*Aside*)

    Surely
    after this
    this Wonderland
    the company will give me
    their favorite son
    on a silver platter
    more responsibilities
    more projects
    more buildings
    of stature
    of rank
    that join rank
    rival those of
    Gehry Wright and Pei

    At long last
    my place in history

At long last
Monuments skyscrapers concert halls

Young Man and Woman applaud. Then Young Man and Woman go to Man and hug him.

MAN   And God's by your side
He's there to guide you
to take care of you
At the end of the day
you'll come back
to a quiet house by the sea
to a charming wife
a beautiful son
and you are home

YOUNG MAN   While the Son is in school
learning his ABC's—

And the hubby
cubbyholed in his skyscraper office—

MAN   Building buildings—

Sound of ESL classroom noise.

YOUNG MAN   The Woman
she takes English classes
at the local university extension
With the usual suspects
a bunch of foreigners
immigrants and exchange students
You know the type—

WOMAN *(To Young Man)*   Ay!
Shh!

Young Man keeps quiet.

WOMAN English as Second Language
Essay
"Why I Love America"

I love America
Yes
I love very much
More than anything else in the world

Everyone
so friendly
Everything here
so clean
so big
Food drink house car ego
all jumbo size
Everything here
just like movies
Exactly like movies

Everyone here
all on improvement kick
diet
exercise
all want to become beautiful skinny blonde
like runaway model

Here
so many opportunities
(that's why I take
English as Second Language class
to speak like real American)

But to live in America
must take more than dream

To survive here
To succeed
you must have strong constipation

No

Sorry
Constitution—
You must have strong constitution

Must hold onto dream
Make no compromise
Your way or no way
If something or someone
threaten dream
seek out problem
and destroy it
immediately!

(*Aside, Softly*)

Must be like me
Survivor
Not like my husband
I come to realize
He is—
what you call?
yes—
he is model minority
Model minority
Always polite
quiet
mister don't-rock-boat
like he is guest
in somebody's house

Don't understand
His family in America
four generations
All working
in Columbus, Ohio
Doctor lawyer engineer architect
But whole family the same
all model people

I will not be
like him
Model minority
I will not be
visitor in this country
I will become owner
A part of this America

(*Brightly*)

What is there not to love
about America?
Everything here wonderful
I smile
because I know
I belong here
This here
is home

End of essay

Young Man and Man applaud.

Sound of ocean.

Woman squints her eyes, looking out into the distance.

MAN   Sometimes I look out
       into the sea
       and wait
       wait

WOMAN   Wait for what?

MAN   Wait for that moment

WOMAN   What moment?

MAN   There

WOMAN   Where?

MAN   There!
       Over there
       Can you see it?

WOMAN   No
         What are you—

MAN   The golden carpet

WOMAN   What carpet where?

         You dreaming again

         Look
         what I got for you today
         Subscription
         Better Homes and Gardens
         So you can be better
         best architect

         Happy?

MAN   Happy

Man and Woman laugh. They hold each other.

         You look nice tonight

329

WOMAN   I love you

MAN   I love you too

WOMAN   You want to?

Beat.

MAN   Yes

Man and Woman kiss.

Sound of ocean.

YOUNG MAN   Years fly by
               The Man and the Son
                       continue the father–son tradition
                       You know
                               the Mr. Cleaver Beaver routine

        Sitting together
            on the deck of the Sandpiper
                in front of the golden carpet
                talking
                    sharing secrets

Man and Son sit together in front of the ocean.

SON   Kids in school
              during break
              during recess
                  they come up
                      run up to me
                      call me

        ching chong chinaman
            ching chong chinaman

        They dance
            around me

                    ching chong Chinaman
                        They dance
                            in vicious circles
                                fingers pointing

        Make their eyes
            almond and slit
                Sometimes I wanna hit
                    Wanna deck them

        But I don't

            Don't understand

                All I hear
                    that refrain
                        that song
                            ching chong chinaman

Silence.

SON   Did that ever happen to—?

MAN   Yes
        Many times—

SON   What did you—?

MAN   Nothing

SON   Nothing?

MAN   I did nothing—

SON   But why?

MAN   There's no point to—

SON   Don't you want to fight—?

Silence.

SON   Is that the right thing?
            Turn the other cheek?

                    Why do you always do the right thing?
                      What's with the right thing?
                            You're always upright polite tight

        You don't know
               but people down the street
                    they nod laugh at you
                        Say you're always the little nice Asian man

                            Always volunteering
                                volunteering at the PTA
                                    volunteering for the
                                        neighborhood watch
                                            Why don't you—

Silence.

Man gets up.

MAN   I've got to get to work

SON   I thought—
               you said
                    we were going
                        to the movies
                            At the Lumiere
                                tonight—

MAN   I can't—

SON   But you promised
               you said—

MAN   I have—

SON   Work

MAN   Yes
           I've got to work late—

SON   Never mind

Man gives Son money.

MAN   Here

> For the movies
> with your friends
> and go buy yourself something
> Good boy

Man leaves.

Son looks at the money.

WOMAN (*To Son*)   In your father's religion
I learn from church
one story

> Abraham love God
> Always listen to God
> So one day God say to Abraham
> "I want you to bring your only son
> make sacrifice for me"

> Because Abraham love God so much
> he bring his son Isaac
> to mountaintop
> for sacrifice

> Just when Abraham about to stab Isaac
> like pork chop steak fries Lea and Perrin sauce
> God said   ′
> "Guess what?
> Just joking
> Only want to test your loyalty"

> Can you imagine
> how Isaac must feel about his father?

For years
Isaac probably spend rest of life
sitting on psychiatrist couch
taking yellow pills

Even God not exempt
He send His only son Jesus
to die for mankind

In His last hours on planet earth
Jesus beg God
"Please let someone else take my place"
And God say
"No sorry I already make will
and My will be done"

God turn away from Jesus
Just like that
Long story short
Jesus become celebrity

Must be patient
Even God have father and son problem

Sound of school bell.

Sound of classroom noises.

YOUNG MAN   A few days later

A high school classroom
Kids
Little no neck monsters
screaming
throwing paper
paper clips
Whispering

Passing love notes
> giggling
>> sleeping
It's the last period of the day

Sound of a school bell ring.

SON Uh—
> I'm next—
>> Miss Alfaro

Son looks at Man.

SON "My Father"
> An essay

My father is an architect
> He built the Wonderland mall
>> You guys know the one
>>> Yeah, isn't that cool?
>>>> But—

Man out, never looking at Son.

MAN (*Warmly*) My father
worked hard and long
because he wanted the very best
for his family
for us—

SON An incessant workaholic
> A man defined by his job—

MAN A man qualified by his work
I hardly saw him when I was growing up—

SON The only image I have of him
he giving me money

his way of saying "I love you"
        compensation for time not spent—

MAN   Here was a man
       who spent the better half of the day
       away from home—

SON   The half of his life
            Mom and I know nothing about
            I mean
                    What's the other half
                    of his life like?—

MAN   The half
       I wasn't privy to
       The half
       he spent in the company
       The half
       he spent talking to Jesus on Sundays—

SON   Who are his colleagues
            his clients
                    his friends?—

MAN   Here was a man
       throughout his whole life
       who believed in the right thing
       in doing the right thing—

SON   Is he happier?
            Is he more attentive?
                    Did he laugh a lot more?—

MAN   Here was a man
       who passionately believed
       in the strength

the power
of the straight line
Model parent
Model citizen—

SON Was he a different person
       than the old man who comes home from work?
         Always tired, always silent?
           Who is he?—

MAN These days
  whenever I look into the mirror
  I see him
  my father

  It's funny
  No matter how far we run away from our fathers
  we end up just like them

Man smiles.

SON I hope this doesn't sound crass or anything
     My dad's a great guy
       But
          I don't want to be my father
            I know you're supposed to wanna grow up
             Be like him
               Follow in his footsteps and stuff

            But
           I don't—
         I can't

           The end
             Any questions?

Sound of ocean.

YOUNG MAN　Meanwhile
　　　　　　　Back on the set
　　　　　　　　more special bonding
　　　　　　　　more QT with Mummy Dearest—

WOMAN　"All the same
　　　　I'll go on loving you
　　　　For as long as I live"

SON (*Rapidly*)　"I love you with the time I have left
　　　　　　　Angela
　　　　　　　　Forget me"

WOMAN　They kiss
　　　　Music
　　　　Music
　　　　Music

　　　　Then Liz Taylor
　　　　in simple black dress—

SON　Can we please just finish up—?

WOMAN　Simple black dress
　　　　White collar—

SON　Yeah yeah yeah
　　　　And her white handkerchief
　　　　　　she keeps twisting twisting twisting
　　　　　　　She walks out of the cell
　　　　　　　　Looks at Montgomery Clift—

Son snaps his fingers to cue Woman.

WOMAN　"Good-bye George　　**SON**　"The best part of
　　　Seems like we only spend　　　　　our time just
　　　The best part of our time　　　　saying goodbye"
　　　Just saying good-bye"

338

SON Blah blah blah
           She zips out of the prison
                Montgomery Clift gets fried and dies
              Fade to black
              The end

    Mom
          I'm going over to George and—

WOMAN One more time—

SON No!—

WOMAN *A Place in the Sun*
        One more time
        Then you can—

SON No!
         I'm already late
           George is—

WOMAN You spend too much time
        with that George hooligan—

SON I don't care—
         I'm going out with—

WOMAN Maybe you not hear me clearly—

Son mimics Woman.

SON Maybe *you* not hear me clearly—

WOMAN You dare speak to me like this—

SON This whole thing is stupid—
        We always—

WOMAN It is not stupid—

SON   This is so fucked—
          I hate this shit—

WOMAN   Don't use words like—

SON   A grown woman like you—
          Playing this pathetic fucked up—

WOMAN   Fine!
            Then don't play!
            Don't need you to play—!

(*Son runs off.*)

WOMAN   Sometimes
            to do something correct
            must do yourself

Sound of ocean.

YOUNG MAN   That same evening
                Dressed in a white slip
                        It's Maggie
                                Cat on a Hot Tin Roof

WOMAN   You so late

MAN   Busy at the office

WOMAN   You work too hard

MAN   Deadlines

WOMAN   Another shopping mall?

MAN   It's lucrative and—

WOMAN   I thought you want to build—

MAN   It's good money—

WOMAN   I remember you said you—

MAN   Yes I know—

WOMAN   Monuments skyscrapers concert halls—

MAN   Why do you always—

WOMAN   I only want best for you

Beat.

MAN   I talked cajoled persuaded them
about giving me
monuments skyscrapers concert halls
to design
to build

But
they laughed
Said no
Said I found my niche
my place
Building malls
Since I built them cheap fast well
why not build more?

I wanted to say no but—

Well—

We have a mortgage
bills to pay—

WOMAN   But you can always ask again—

MAN   So where's the boy?

Beat.

WOMAN   As usual
go out
with his friend George
Probably at the mall

MAN   He's growing up fast

WOMAN   Wish he do better in school
Always running around
Never home
Never study
All C's, all D's
With grades like these
how can go to college?
How he can be doctor lawyer engineer architect?
I don't know what to do with him

MAN   I'll speak to him

Beat.

MAN   You look nice tonight

Man and Woman kiss.

WOMAN   I love you

MAN   I love you too

WOMAN   You want to?

MAN   I'm—tired—

Beat.

WOMAN   Me too
Tired

Beat.

342

MAN Bed?

Beat.

WOMAN Bed

Woman lies down and sleeps.

Man looks at her.

MAN God by your side
       A quiet house by the sea
       A charming wife
       A beautiful son
       Welcome to the rest of your life

       How did we become
       so decidedly middle-aged?
       Was it so many moons ago
       so many beds ago
       that we were lying side by side
       planning extraordinary lives?

(Man looks away from Woman.)

       Is this it?
       The Wonderland mall
       Have I reached my paramount
       my peak?

       And you stand on this peak
       alone
       thinking there's more
       More peaks
       more trophies
       So
       like a fool
       you continue to climb

you reach
with grubby hands
grabbing
clutching at air
at watered-down fantasies
at paper-thin dreams
at
nothingness

In the end
with your solitary face
towards the claustrophobic sky
you face
your own mediocrity
you face
your own mortality
you face
yourself
and
it's cold
there
in the shadow of the man
you thought you were meant to be

Man lies down and sleeps.

Woman gets up and looks at him.

WOMAN   My husband
He is dreamer
A man with big dream

There is nothing wrong with dream
Except he want all his dream
to come true

Sometimes
He not home

or he in bed
I go to his study
Open
Unroll all his drawings
and look at them
Just like I look at them
first time
back in Singapore

*Woman shows the audience a drawing. Drawing can be illustrated by
a box of light on the stage floor.*

Look
Look at his drawing
He draw all this incredible building
This incredible
magnificent building
So beautiful
So special
But no one
can build it
No one
want to build it
Why?
Because building too expensive
Too different
Too imaginative
for an unimaginative world

And he give up?
No
He keep on drawing
He keep on designing for client
Client who don't care
Client who only want

cheap quick and big
Client who only want same thing
same buildings
like all other building in city

So
you stand by him
through thick
through thin

Listen to his dream like
you hear them for first time
like you know his dream will come true
Because you are wife
Because you love him

Look at his drawings
Look at his dreams

This is map
to his heart

Sound of seventies pop music.

YOUNG MAN   Plastered
                    along on the walls
        Glossy posters
            Shaun Cassidy
                    Leif Garrett and *Star Wars*
                        Glossy posters
            ripped out from the bible of teenagers
                    Sixteen magazine
        The floor is strewn
                    with vinyl records
                    books clothes tennis rackets junk

                        You've guessed it

My bedroom
                at the Sandpiper

        Two kids playing
                playacting

SON "Well, one must be serious about something, if one
     wants to have any amusement in life. I happen to be
     serious about—"
                "Serious about—"

        Shit
                Don't tell me
                        "Serious about—"
                                Damn

Okay
        Tell me
                What comes after—
                        "Bunburying"
                                Of course
                                        "Bunburying"

I'm such a schmuck
        Can't get it into my head
                I'll never get this right
                        How will I memorize
                                this whole damn thing?

I wanna act
        Be an actor
                Be a movie star
                        Don't want to be a doctor lawyer
                        engineer architect
                                Like what my folks want me to do
                                I got my life
                                        They got theirs

347

It's so fucked
        I just wanna live a full life
                You know
                        With no regrets

I want to live
        A full life
                A complete life
                        Not some half life
                                A full life
                                        Or nothing at all

I want—
        I want—
                I want so so much—
                        I want everything

George
        You think we'll ever get there?
                I mean really
                        Really get there
                                To that
                                        That beyond
                                                Wherever the fuck it is

Let's start again George
        I want to get it right
                From the top
                        From the beginning

                                "Well, one must be serious about
                                something, if one wants to have any
                                amusement in life"

Woman to Man. She refers to Son. Man does nothing.

WOMAN Ay
        Speak to him

Look
look at him
Not good in school
Not bright
Fail most classes
He only likes sissy subjects
Art
History
Literature
What use
art in life?

Think we send him to school
spend money on him
only to become actor
and live on welfare?
I don't think so

At this rate
how can he be
doctor lawyer engineer architect?
How can he be success?

Ay
Talk to him

He is always
how you say?
nuisance

He play music
very loud
smoke funny-smelling cigarette

SON   It's pot

WOMAN   Never come home
Dye his hair

think he is rock star
black hair dye blond

(*Woman to Son*)

What you are?
Robert Redford blond?

SON No
Marilyn Monroe blonde

WOMAN (*Out*) I pretend not to hear
Don't say anything
A son like that
What to do?
Have to discipline
Have to beat
Beat until behave
Beat until good

Woman goes to Son and grabs his hair.

Cut it—

SON No
Let go—

WOMAN You cut hair
Or I cut for you—

SON I said
Let go—

WOMAN Cut
Or dye it black again—

SON Let go of my hair—

WOMAN You hear?—

SON No!

No!

No!

WOMAN You answer back?
You dare answer back?

Woman slaps Son. Son glares at Woman.

SON Don't you ever
ever
do that again!

Son storms off.

WOMAN You see your son changing
in front of your eyes
Becoming someone you don't know

Sometimes it's better
to slip into shadow
into silence

In the end
He in his world
I in mine

Sound of mall traffic.

YOUNG MAN Time passes
We find ourselves in Wonderland

At one end of the mall
The Son and his best friend George
hanging out
in a quiet unpopulated
corner of the food court

351

On the other end
        the Woman sits on bench
                armed with purchases
                    exhausted from a day of frenetic shopping

WOMAN I realize my life here
not like American movies
More like foreign-language film
But without subtitles

Back in Singapore
I always think
if I live in America
I will have friends
Close friends like sisters
Just like Liz Taylor in *Little Women*

But once I open my mouth
people treat me
more like
Liz Taylor in *Suddenly Last Summer*

When I keep talking
I see in their face
They don't know what I am talking about
Even though I try
very hard
to speak my better best English
English I learn from ESL class

Worse is
People all nod
All smile at me
Then they walk away

SON George?
    Listen
        I was thinking

                    Wondering
                         I mean
                              When you see me
                                   Think about me even

          What do you see?
               I mean
                    You see a friend?
                         Someone you hang with?
                              Or

                                   Or some Asian guy?
                                        Of course I know
                                             I can't change that
          But is it an issue?
               I mean—
                    Well—

WOMAN   I realize
               no matter how many English class I take
               I will never speak like real American
               So why waste money?
               Why waste time?

               So instead
               I come here
               to Wonderland mall
               Look at shop window
               Go shopping
               Go cineplex
               Eat lunch in food court
               every day

               Here in mall
               you have everything
               All shiny and new
               Big and modern

I like it here
Wonderland
my second home

SON Just now
I was walking
Outside the mall
And some guy
Some homeless guy
came up to me
asking for change
I had none
told him

And he called me
a Jap
I said I'm not a Jap
Then
he called me
a Chink
I said I'm not a Chink
I'm American

But he didn't hear nothing
kept on calling me
Gook! Gook! Gook!
I even thought
I'd give him a dollar
just to shut him up
But before I knew it
I decked the
asshole
Square on
the chin

354

           I mean
                I may look Asian
                     But I'm not like Asian or anything
                          You know
                               I'm not

WOMAN   In mall
                I always go to Macy's department store
                Cosmetic counter
                Try new Max Factor
                Lipstick blush eyeliner
                Pretend to buy something

                I smile
                I say to Mexican salesgirl
                "You know
                my husband
                he built this mall"

                But Mexican salesgirl
                She smile
                Look at me
                Like little child
                dying of cancer

                I smile
                Tell her again
                This time very slowly
                Who—build—mall

                Again
                She smile
                She say
                "Nice color for lipstick
                no?"

With answer like that
you wonder why
she not employee of the month

Anyway
I get fed up
Smile charge sign
Buy lipstick
Take bus
RTD
go home

Tomorrow
determined
I come back
And remind them who build mall

Tomorrow
like movie say
is another day

SON   I'm American
            American as anyone else
                  Right?
                        Hey

                  Bet you didn't know
                        I hate Asians
                              Yeah
                                    Really
                                          Swear to God

You see them in school in the streets you know
      Always like in groups and stuff
            Smoking cigarettes
                  Playing with computers

Always loud obnoxious
And the way they talk
Laughing in some strange
fucking language

Christ!
Learn fucking English man!
And all I have is this face
This face
that kinda—

I mean—
I have nothing in common with them
Nothing

Nothing

This conversation is so screwed
Let's not—
I don't know why—
It was just bugging me

Thanks for letting me—
Letting me talk—
Yeah—

Listen George
I like hanging with you
Really
I'm glad we're friends
and—

(*Son closes his eyes like he is being kissed.*)

Wow
Shit
No
I'm not

357

I wanted it too
I wanted it so long
to do this
with you

Wow
Hey
George
I'm
I'm so happy

Kiss
Kiss me
Yeah
Again
Again
and again

Woman walks into Son's side of the mall.

Woman sees Son and is shocked. Son opens his eyes in surprise. They look at each other for a beat.

SON Mom
What are you—

WOMAN Marilyn Monroe blonde

Woman walks away quickly.

SON Shit
I
Uh
Hey man
Don't worry about it
George
Don't freak

It's
            It's okay
                Let me
                    I'll deal with it
    Fuck

Son runs away.

Sound of bar chatter and noise.

YOUNG MAN   Welcome to La Cucaracha
                            You know the bar
                        tucked away
                    in some quiet street corner
                                musty dark and dank

            the clack clack crack
    of billiard balls
                strained guitar riffs
            classic Springsteen on the wailing jukebox
                Moldy stench of
                            cheap cigarettes and booze

(*Young Man assumes role of a bartender.*)

        Regulars
                they cluster at the bar
                            nursing the wounds of life

                                Late afternoon
                    and someone is being a naughty boy—

MAN   I play hooky from work
    some afternoons
    Head across the street to a bar
    where I'd sit
    with another double scotch on the rocks
    Eating stale peanuts

Watching a droning baseball game
on a beat-up TV set overhead

My mind invariably drifts
I wonder why I'm doing what I'm doing?
And should I?
since the glass ceiling is only so high?

Suddenly
a news bulletin
it pulls me back to the real world
A middle-aged woman with a bad permanent
She says
there is a disaster
a tragedy
Armageddon
The governor
the mayor
every elected public official
all appear on the screen
Speaking in an election voice
"State of emergency, disaster area, crisis"
they say
"Our hearts, our sympathies, our thoughts"
they say
"Terrorist attacks, bombs, Arabs"
they say
I stop hearing what they say

I stand
like everyone else in the bar
transfixed
intoxicated
An image of destruction
a building

its roof punctured
crumpled
fallen

The woman with a bad permanent
she interrupts
Roof collapse
Structural failure
Shoddy construction
Death toll high
still climbing

The woman with a bad permanent
she says
the building
is
the Wonderland mall

My mall

I don't hear anymore

Man runs off.

Sound of pandemonium, sirens and people yelling.

YOUNG MAN   A car lunging
   hurtling on Interstate 5
         The Man
      he drives
   like a maniac
      at breakneck speed
            to the mall—

In another corner of the stage, Woman looks at Man.

WOMAN   I come home
      Look at him

Nothing to say
What to say?—

MAN When I arrive
the pungent smell
of burning wood metal brick greets me—

YOUNG MAN The Man
he stands small
against the looming mall
The devastated part of the building
the food court
is surrounded
by wailing ambulances
fire engines
cranes—

MAN I stand there
paralyzed
not knowing where to run
where to turn
right or left
I just stand there
Staring—

WOMAN He stand there
Silent
Defeated—

YOUNG MAN Like a site of a ravenous war
in defeat
retreat
In the distance
raging amber flames
consume the food market
Walls stained black by soot and fire—

362

MAN I notice
    the rest of the mall remains standing
    as if in defiance—

WOMAN You do what wife supposed to do
    Be understanding
    Listen
    Hold him
    But he push you away
    Don't tell you a thing—

YOUNG MAN Pandemonium
        Thick in the bilious smoke
        A towering babble
          Howling sirens
    People running standing
        People screaming crying—

MAN I want to rush forward
    to help them
    but I don't
    I can't
    Instead
    I just keep staring
    at the mall
    my beautiful mall—

YOUNG MAN Outside the mall
    People fearful
      hopeful
    for their loved ones
        trapped deep in the rubble—

SON The day it happened
    I got home from school

I saw on TV
           Body bags on the streets
                   Like it's Beirut or Bosnia
                           Bombed-out buildings and stuff
                           Wild

YOUNG MAN   Rescue workers and their dogs
                           rummage through
                   twisted steel
                           fractured concrete
                                   for signs of life
                           any life—

WOMAN   Outside
           He just stand in balcony
           Don't look at me
           Ignore me
           Looking at ocean—

MAN   The rescue workers
           they say
           they hear voices—
           voices praying for God

           But a few hours later
           their prayers
           stop—

Son enters.

SON   When I saw him
           Dad on TV
                   A middle-aged woman with a bad permanent
                   She says it's his mistake
                           his fault
                                   the roof collapsed

For a moment
    I want to speak to him
        Say something
            But what's there really to say?
                Especially when everything's being
                said on TV?

      He has my father's voice
          His face his posture his size
              But yet it isn't him
                    He's someone else

WOMAN   Inside
I see him
My husband
on TV
A middle-aged woman with bad permanent
She say it's his mistake
his fault
the roof collapse

For a moment
I want to speak to him
say something
But what to say?
Especially when everything's being said on TV?—

YOUNG MAN   Television newspaper reporters
        they aim
                point in Dad's direction
    They make a run towards him
            Armed with cameras lights sound
      They blind him—

Man shields his eyes from the lights.

Young Man and Woman surround Man. They batter him with an endless barrage of questions.

SON (*Overlapping*)   Are you accountable for the
                                                  collapse of the roof?—

MAN (*Overlapping*)   No—no—

WOMAN (*Overlapping*)   Did you know—?
                                              Were you—?

MAN (*Overlapping*)   No—no charges of negligence
                                              have been filed against me—

YOUNG MAN (*Overlapping*)   Did you know the civil engineer
    has corroborated with federal
                  authorities?—

WOMAN (*Overlapping*)   Are you—?
                                              Why did you—?

SON (*Overlapping*)   Was it a bad judgement call?

MAN (*Overlapping*)   No—no—
                                          I don't intend to sell my story
                                          to *60 Minutes*—
                                          No interviews—

YOUNG MAN (*Overlapping*)   A fatal miscalculation?—

WOMAN (*Overlapping*)   Are you—?
                                              Why could you—?
                                              Why did you—?

YOUNG MAN (*Overlapping*)   Are you a murderer?—
    Charges of manslaughter—

MAN (*Overlapping*)   No—no—
                                          I'm not a murderer—

SON (*Overlapping*)   Do you know you are subpoenaed?
                          Your architectural license has been—

MAN (*Overlapping*)   Not a murderer—

YOUNG MAN (*Overlapping.*)   Sixteen lives have been lost—

SON (*Overlapping*)   Men—women—children—

WOMAN (*Overlapping*)   Why didn't you—?
                            How can you—?
                            Look at you—

MAN   Not a murderer!
          not a murderer!
          not a murderer!

Silence.

MAN (*Softly*)   Oh God

                     Sixteen
                     Sixteen lives
                     Sixteen innocents
                     And some of them
                     children

                     I—
                     didn't mean to—
                     I mean—
                     you know—
                     I didn't—
                     didn't mean to—

                     It's not my fault—
                     not my—
                     you know that
                     right?

                     Right?

WOMAN   He just stand there
Alone
So I stand next to him
Together alone
we look out at balcony
until sun
sky
ocean
All turn black

SON   He has my father's voice
His face his posture his size
But yet it isn't him
He's someone else

Young Man looks at Man.

YOUNG MAN   Christ
What a loser

Sound of bar chatter and noise.

Young Man assumes role of bartender. He gives Man a drink.

YOUNG MAN   Later that same day
in the black night
back in La Cucaracha

MAN   I find myself
back in the comfort of the quiet bar
glad to see the TV set above
turned off
But I can still see
in the dark vacant screen
a building
its heart
collapsed

reduced
to sand and rubble

I gulp down
another double scotch on the rocks

(*Apathetically*)

And thank God
thank Him
that I still have a wife
a son
and a place to call home

PART TWO

WOMAN   The other day
I see butterfly
Monarch butterfly
with pretty red wing
Red
like color of falling sun
in winter morning

I see butterfly outside
slowly flying
near window
Butterfly hovering
wondering
if it should fly into house

House feel
warm
cozy
colorful
Much better than outside life

So
curious and excited
this uninvited visitor
cross border
burst into house

It fly
Migrate from
room to room

Explore
baby blue walls of room

Dance around
the big red couch
Rest on
teak table
Feast on bright tremendous color
of big painting

It was in heaven

After a while
Monarch butterfly
got tired of flying around
like leisure tourist on big bus

So butterfly
decide to leave the house
for it long to see
outside world again
It long to fly
free and high
rest on sweet pollen flowers
dance to day of spring

So butterfly
again it fly
search room to room
for the same window
it come in from

But confused
Monarch butterfly
cannot find window
Cannot find way back

It was lost
It had no map to window

So
butterfly fly around
like mad
Desperate for outside sky

Suddenly
the butterfly find window
window of sky

But different window
shut window

Butterfly
not notice
Joyous
it fly straight
into window

Bang!

Its little head hit
against glass pane
Surprised and confused
butterfly
can see the outside
can recognize
warm glow of sunlight
can see blue expanse of sky
The world it came in from

But
somehow
something is blocking butterfly

Desperate to be a part of outside
butterfly try
again

and again
bang its little head
against glass

Frantic
again
and again

Infuriated
Harder
and harder
until blood
pour out of its head
pour over its little compound eyes
blinding butterfly

Butterfly
not give up
not give in

It try
again
and again

But
even its tired wings
fluttering madly
cannot carry butterfly
into clear open

I just stand there
Don't know why I don't open window
Stand there
Looking at butterfly
Feeling sorry
Admiring
determination of butterfly

Its faded red wing
flutter
slow
up
and
down
flicker
like dying sunlight

Then
butterfly
exhausted and dying
lie still
on windowsill

A day later
butterfly die
die of crush head
of exhaustion
of heartache

But
butterfly
still has head
pointing toward outside
outside
where it once belong

I pick up dead butterfly
Its powdered wings
Crumble upon touch

I walk outside to balcony
Throw the butterfly
out

And
I see it
fly
once more
once again
for a moment
for brief moment
downward spiral
into deep blue sea below

● Then
it disappear
into ocean

Sound of ocean roar.

YOUNG MAN   A blur

Seconds minutes days weeks
they pass

Everyone tries to return
to their own individual lives
in their own individual ways

The Man
Mister Successful American Architect
does what guilty parties do best

He returns to the scene of the crime
time and time
again

MAN   I find myself
back in Wonderland
A sea of rubble stone and twisted steel

In this wreckage
I see my dreams
My work as an architect
like pieces
on the ground
in pieces
unrecognizable
irretrievable

(*Man gets down on his knees.*)

I get on my knees
With my bare hands
I try to piece back
the broken tiles
the torn wood beams
the smashed glass pieces
piecing back
a broken mall

It's futile

I look at
my hands

bloody

wet

red

Sound of ocean.

YOUNG MAN   And when he returns home—

(*Man standing and looking out into the audience.*)

The Man
　　　　he stands at the balcony
　　　　　　　　looking at the ocean

376

looking looking
at the endless blue

(*Woman looks at man.*)

Inside the Sandpiper
the Woman
She sits quietly
in the living room
keeping an ever vigilant
ever watchful eye on the Man

WOMAN My husband
He keep a lot to himself
since mall fall down

Every day he go to work
And when he come home
he smell of alcohol
He never talk
never touch me

I want to reach out
Say something
Do something
But I don't know how

One time
I open my mouth
I ask him

(*To Man*)

"You okay?"

Beat.

Man is silent, not looking at Woman but at the ocean in front of him.

377

WOMAN He say nothing

    I ask him
    "You hungry?"

Beat.

Man is silent, not looking at Woman but at the ocean in front of him.

WOMAN He say nothing

    Then
    I ask him
    "Is it true
    what they say about you
    on TV
    in newspaper
    did you—?"

MAN No—

WOMAN He—

MAN Not responsible—

WOMAN He—

MAN Didn't do anything

WOMAN He—

    He say nothing more
    His eyes looking at ocean
    Eyes never at me

    Sometimes
    I feel invisible

YOUNG MAN Meanwhile
    in another corner of the Sandpiper

                the Son and his "best friend" George
                            continue
                         to spend time
                      continue
                         to spend a lifetime
                                    of afternoons
                            daydreaming
                                    dreaming

Sound of ocean.

SON   My dad?
              He—
                    I haven't said a thing—
                         Don't know what to say—
                         He's been —

      Listen
           George
              I've been thinking about—
                   Well—

George
      Let's chuck quit school
         Leave home
            Do our own thing
               Live our own lives
                  Life is too short

We can get our own place
      Somewhere in the hills
            like you always wanted
               white picket fence
                  the works and
                        we can do it super nice—

Remember the magic carpet?
          Running to great beyond?
               We can do it
                    I know I'm still losing you
                         with this carpet stuff
                              But
                                   can't you see?

(*Beat*)

    Why not?

Well
          Just think about it
               Okay?
                    Think about it

What?
          Speak to him?
               Dad?
                    I don't know what to—
                         We don't speak like we used to and—

    I don't even know
          if Mom said anything to him about—
               That day at the mall when she—
                    Two of us—
                         I think he's—

    I don't know

Sound of ocean.

Man looks up in the sky.

MAN   I don't know
          the words to say

the words to conjure
the words to right a wrong

What can I earthly give
to recompense
What can I sacrifice
to rectify
all that happened
in one fell swoop
a coffin
a roof
made for sixteen?

My passion
mission
My obsession
possession
to create
to build
now one of destruction

Amend everything
My wrong right
My bent marrow straight
All my dreams a reality

And I will again
walk and toe
Your straight and narrow
Tend the way
Your words have intended

Give me
again Your hand
and let me
again build

And
in turn
I will give You anything
to remedy
everything

Son enters.

Son sits next to Man like the way they used to in part 1 of the play.

SON Dad?
           Are you—

MAN It was an accident
          Everything's being taken care of

SON You can tell me what happened—

MAN Nothing happened

Beat.

SON Okay

Silence.

MAN I am glad
          we can do this again

          Two of us
          Here

          Sitting in front of the ocean
          Toes dangling in the salt air
          Talking
          Father to son

          It's been some time
          And—

SON   Yes
                    It has been some time

Beat.

SON   Dad?

MAN   Yes?

SON   I—

MAN   What?

SON   I've been thinking—

MAN   About?

SON   College

MAN   Good

SON   No I mean—
                    I'm thinking about leaving school—

MAN   Leave school?—

SON   I wanna go into acting—

MAN   You have to finish high school first—

SON   You're not listening—

MAN   Then college—

SON   I have it all figured out—

MAN   What kind of life—

SON   We'll get our own place—

MAN   Who's we?

SON   Me and George—

MAN   You and George—

SON   Dad
               That's what I need to talk to you about

Silence.

MAN   What?

SON   George and me
                 We—

Silence.

SON   George means the world to—
               Dad—
                           I don't how to say this to you—

MAN   You are—

SON   I am—

Man looks away from Son and once again stares at the ocean.

MAN   Leviticus twenty thirteen

SON   Dad?

MAN   Leviticus twenty thirteen—

SON   What
                   What are you—?

MAN   Leviticus twenty thirteen—

SON   Can we—?

MAN   Leviticus twenty thirteen—

SON   Why do you keep saying—?

MAN   Leviticus twenty thirteen—

SON   Dad
             Speak normal to me
                          Please?

MAN   Leviticus twenty thirteen—

SON   Dad
             Please let me explain
                          George and me—

MAN   Leviticus twenty thirteen—

SON   Dad please—

MAN   Leviticus twenty thirteen—

SON   Why are you—
             Speak to me—
                    Please—

MAN   Leviticus twenty thirteen—

SON   What's—?

MAN   Leviticus twenty thirteen—

SON   What's Leviticus twenty thirteen, Dad?

MAN   "If a man lies with a man
       as one lies with a woman
       both of them have done
       what is detestable
       they must be put to death
       their blood
       will be on their heads"
       Leviticus twenty thirteen

Pause.

SON Leviticus
              twenty
         thirteen

*Son looks at Man. Son runs. Man doesn't look at Son. Man looks
up at the sky.*

YOUNG MAN (*Laughs*)   The Man
              He mutters the magic verse
                        and sets everything in motion

                              Even then
              he didn't really do anything

                              Lucky for him
                    the Son did

                              Now he has no son

Sound of street traffic.

YOUNG MAN That same night
              We find ourselves
                    in the heart of heartless Hollywood

                    On the bustling streets
         impatient Hondas meandering
                              BMWs zooming
                    Volvos honking

    On the hustling pavements
                    people of all shapes and colors
                              talking
                                    walking
                         baiting

          waiting

               And in the midst of it all—

Son runs.

SON   So you run
           from home
      Run
        run far
          run free
     Like the wind
   flash zip
       wishing for the golden carpet
           Only it fails you
  like everything usually does

          So you stuff a couple shirts
           flannels
       a couple of 501s
            white tees
          seventy dollars
      Pack them all
    in a backpack
      and run

It was time
     anyways
       to leave
         Gotta go
           See the world
       Do the world

No matter how far you run
     You can always hear

                    yelling
                always yelling
                        Mom

                                        yelling

WOMAN How could you?—
           Why did you?—

Son looks at Woman. Woman looks out. Son laughs and mocks her.

SON Finger-pointing—

SON "You couldn't be"   **WOMAN** You couldn't be!
  "No"   No!
  "Can't"   Can't!
  I hear   Not possible!
  every word   No son of mine!
  yelling   What will people say?
  saying   What will neighbors
  Every word   say?
  Sentence phrase   Why you turn out like
  Everything she says the way   this?
  she speaks an endless   Ay, you deaf or what?
  soundtrack of broken English   Ay, you listening or
  Embarrasses the fuck outta me   not?
  Always telling me what to do   Why you like this?
  Saying she wanted me to be   Why?
  something   Better be someone
  she can be proud of   else's son!
  Wanted me to be   If you cannot be
  doctor lawyer engineer architect doctor lawyer
                                    engineer
                                    architect!

SON   All I see
        in the middle of the room
                    a middle-aged frump
                            talking like a boat person
                    finger wagging
                            yelling
                    Her eyes
        unwavering
                    unforgiving
                            She was glad to see me go
            glad to see me run

                    So I run
                        run far
                            run free

(*Son to Man sadly. Man out.*)

    And no matter how far you run
                    you see him
                there
                in his predictable corner
                        in the comfort of shadows
            while she rants she raves
                        His head hung low
            eyes looking at the balcony
                the ocean
                        looking at the ocean
                        and
                            not at me
                                    Standing—

MAN   Trapped—

SON   Small—

MAN   Suffocated—

SON   Frightened—

MAN   Scrambling
        for the right words
        to say—

SON   To him

MAN   Your son—

SON   Your father—

MAN   You want to say
        It's all right—

SON   You can understand where he's coming from
                You can forgive—

MAN   But your mind
        it does not dance
        with your heart—

SON   You should have expected
           should have known—

MAN   The words that
        spew automatic
        from your mouth—

SON   Are not ones of comfort
               of embrace
        but ones that wound—

MAN   That sting

        Your own mortal words
        replaced by
        God's immortal ones—

SON   And what mortal words can you say
              to Dad
                    to rival God's?

MAN   You were taught—

SON   Right and wrong—

MAN   Black and white—

SON   Good and bad—

MAN   You were taught—

SON   This is the way—

MAN   The way
        it has always been—

SON   It's all shit
                 It's all fucked—

MAN   What happens when everything
        that you know
        that you believe in
        turns
        into a sudden gray—?

SON   Suddenly
                  you can't
         you don't
              see the grays anymore
           Everything makes sense
                    perfect sense
           Everything's crystal clear—

MAN   Where do you stand?
        In God's harsh light
        or in His cool cool shadow—?

SON You feel a sudden jolt
a rush
It's jubilation
joy
This must be what freedom tastes like
Yeah
This must be what happiness feels like
And it feels good—

MAN What would you do?
What could you do—?

SON And suddenly
you know what to do—

MAN So
you say what you say
to him
Your son—

SON Suddenly
it's easy—

Son raises his hands into the air.

MAN And the rest
is easy—

SON So I run
run far
run free

Son runs off.

Sound of ocean.

WOMAN You not like your dinner—?

MAN Dinner—?

WOMAN Made your favorite again—

MAN Yes
         Pork chops steak fries Lea and Perrin sauce

Pause.

WOMAN How come you not eating?

MAN I'm not hungry

WOMAN You eat already?

MAN No

Pause.

WOMAN Ay
         You think too much
         The mall again?

MAN Can you not talk about it?

WOMAN Your son
         I think about him too

MAN Don't

(*Pause*)

MAN They suspended me
         the company
         from working on future projects

         Suspended me
         until the inquiry
         the investigation is complete

         They suspended me
         to an empty room

with empty walls
Empty papers

Beat.

MAN What's that?

WOMAN What?

MAN Did you hear that?

WOMAN Hear what?

MAN A sound
Outside

Man looks out of window.

MAN Maybe he's outside
Maybe he's come back

WOMAN Who?

MAN Him

Woman and Man look outside window.

WOMAN I don't see him

Woman holds Man.

I love you

MAN I love you too

Beat.

WOMAN Listen
maybe we spend some time together—

MAN Holiday?—

WOMAN If you want

MAN   We haven't gone
in a long time

WOMAN   We can go somewhere
Stay in hotel
Do nothing—

MAN   Make love—

WOMAN   Yes—

MAN   Gin slings—

WOMAN   Go somewhere—

MAN   Somewhere far away—

WOMAN   Yes
Somewhere far away

Pause.

MAN   Listen

About Wonderland

Pause.

WOMAN   Yes?

MAN   I have to tell you something

Pause.

WOMAN   What?

MAN   I

I adjusted the designs
changed it
slightly
made construction more cost-efficient

I chose
I imported
more expensive materials
Italian marble teak wood titanium
I skimmed
compromised on the rest

"Come in on time"
the company said
"Come in on budget"
they chimed
"No overhead"
"Build it quick"
"Just build the mall quick"
they said

And I did
for the company

I did—

WOMAN   For yourself

MAN   No

WOMAN   You responsible—

MAN   I am not—

WOMAN   How can you not be?
Why you do this?

MAN   What do you think pays for this house?
The clothes you wear?
The food you eat?
What do you think you—

WOMAN Blood money—

MAN Don't you—

WOMAN People die and you—

MAN I didn't plan it that way—
I didn't think—

WOMAN You kill these people!

MAN All I saw were monuments skyscrapers—

WOMAN All you saw!—

MAN Yes!—

WOMAN No dream worth that
No dream—

MAN I'm not responsible
Not responsible—

WOMAN Then who responsible?

Who?

God?

Long silence.

Man falls on the ground and holds woman very tightly.

MAN Do you still love me?

Silence.

Woman looks out.

WOMAN Let's go somewhere far
Far away

YOUNG MAN   And as far away
                                                as the Woman wants to be
                                                        she finds herself
                                        solitary
                                finds herself
            within the suffocating four walls of a lonely house

                                        Wondering
            how to love the man she once knew in her absent husband
                                        Wondering
                                                        how her son is

                                Wondering
                                        where he is
                                Wondering
                                        if this is all there is

                                        Wondering
                                in wonderment

(*Sound of park traffic*)

            She takes to taking trips
                            somewhere far far away
                                        from the Sandpiper
                                far far away
                                        from the rest of the world

WOMAN   After six months
                    Wonderland
                    now reopen

                    Roof in food court
                    all repaired
                    Wonderland look like new
                    Look like nothing happen

People who come here
now fewer
Shops use to be very busy
Many of them
now vacant

But
I cannot go back to mall
Too many salesgirl over there
Too many salesgirl
know who build mall
Too many salesgirl
know my husband build mall

So instead
every Thursday
I go to County Museum
Look at paintings
improve myself
study American art and culture

My favorite
in museum
is Rodin
They have room
all devoted to his statues
One statue I really like
called *The Kiss*
Man
woman
in embrace
kissing
Just like Elizabeth Taylor
in *A Place in the Sun*

How can something so lifeless
be so passionate?

I wonder
for a moment
I wonder what is like
to be kissed by these statues
to be touched
by them
To be made love to
by one of these
lifelike
lifeless
statues

So
when no one is in room
I quickly climb onto statue
Touch Rodin's soft hard hands
and kiss his lips
Gently
And like I expect
His lips
Soft
Sensual
Electric

I sigh
fluster
get a little wet

(*Young Man assumes the role of the museum security guard and bursts in.*)

Suddenly security guard
he come into room
He frown

Quickly
I say
"Just studying statue
Sorry
Maybe study too close"

Embarrassed
I leave
nod at security guard
and wait at bus stop
take bus home

All the way home
I think about Rodin
and his large hands
with a big smile
on my face

Sound of office noises.

YOUNG MAN   Downtown Los Angeles
                                 drowns
                                            in heat dust and smog

                            The sun's glaring rays
                        kissing
                            the silver
                                        sliver of a building
                and on the seventeenth floor
        Peterson Peterson and Peterson

                                Clutching his morning brew
                        the Man shuffles
                    towards the glass doors

                                He parts the doors

Says his regular "good morning"
        to Sharon the receptionist
                                and—

MAN   One of the partners
           Peterson
           he stops me
           in the office hallway
           He tells me
           that my architectural license
           has been revoked
           Revoked in light of the investigations
           Peterson
           He tells me it's all over
           Good luck
           Good-bye

(*Young Man assumes the role of Sam the security guard.*)

           Sam
           the black security guard
           he stands next to Peterson
           Sam
           whom I've known for more than twenty years
           Sam
           with whom I've shared an occasional smoke
           an occasional joke
           Sam
           he's waiting to escort me out of the building

           I dig deep
           into my pockets
           retrieve
           a shiny set of office keys
           fish out

the company ID
company credit card
company executive washroom key
place them
in Sam's impatient outstretched palm

Sam
he hands me
a box
I don't look
Don't bother
Only one thing
sticks in my mind

Where's my bonsai?
I want my bonsai

I want my bonsai
a prize
a token
the company has given me
for twenty years
of unrelenting
top-notch
tip-top service
Is this what you get
after all these years
for playing by the book
by the rules?

I want my bonsai
I want my bonsai
And I want it now

Sam
he doesn't hear me

Maybe he doesn't choose to
He's checking the keys
Making sure none were missing

I want my bonsai

(*Man yells.*)

Where is my bonsai!
I want my bonsai!
They gave me that bonsai!

(*Young Man gives Man the bonsai plant.*)

I walk out
into the cold office hallways
A quiet army of unmoving statues
my colleagues
the Petersons
they send me off
Their parade of silent eyes
salute me
I clutch
my wilting bonsai
a brown box of scattered pencil drawings
of buildings never built—

And thank God
thank Him that I have a wife
a son—

(*Expressionlessly*)

And a place to call home

Sound of street traffic.

YOUNG MAN Far far away
from home

                    the Son finds himself
                  back at the same place

            A street corner
                        in glamorous glittering
                  Hollywood

                        Dusk

SON   And you run
                  run far
                        run free
      until your seventy dollars
                  trickle down to seventy cents
                              So you pawn your watch
                  your class ring
                              your GameBoy
            Sold
         to a man in a glass booth
                                    for change
                  Your white tees
      501s
                  backpack
            Sold
      to street pedestrians
                  for more change
      Nope
Can't go home
      Don't wanna go home
                  No home no run-down shelters for you
                  You do what you gotta do
      with what you have
                  You make do
                        with what you are given
                              And you do

On the other side of the stage.

MAN   Here

WOMAN   What is this?

MAN   Bonsai

WOMAN   For what
this bonsai?

MAN   For decoration

WOMAN   How was your day?

MAN   Okay
Yours?

WOMAN   Today I go to museum—

On the other side of the stage.

SON   So you listen
unexpectedly
to life lessons from a ranting mother
Put to practice what she taught you
Be a survivor

She crossed her ocean
and you crossed yours

Aren't you proud of me, mom?
Huh?
I learned everything you taught me
Learned it to the tee
Learned it to the max
Your perfect little actor

I'm a survivor

                                    like you
                                    Mom

                           A fucking survivor

                          So you run
                     run far
                  run free
                          You only run so far
            before you end up here
                           Corner of La Brea and Santa Monica
            Looking for a friend
                     who gives you
                            a little wad
                            That
                                    and a wad of green
            In fifteen minutes half hour whatever
                                    will kiss you like George did
                            And for a little more green
            will make clumsy love like he did

On the other side of the stage.

WOMAN   So you want dinner?
            I can make for—

MAN   No I am not—

WOMAN   No problem
            I can—

MAN   Forget it—

WOMAN   Pork chops steak fries Lea and Perrin sauce—

MAN   I don't want
            pork chops steak fries Lea and Perrin sauce—

WOMAN   You always like to—

MAN   No—
    I never liked the—

WOMAN   You always eat and—

MAN   You always make it every—

WOMAN   Then don't eat I—

MAN   And I always eat it—

WOMAN   I don't make next time then—

MAN   Fine

On the other side of the stage.

SON   Sometimes an angel appears
                    he'll buy you a burger
    a messy taco and a lukewarm Coke
                    Maybe a special treat
            pork chops steak fries Lea and Perrin sauce
        And if he's nice
                    really nice
                            gentle
                    smells good
        I may even let him
                    without protection
                            Says it feels better
        I want him to feel better

On the other side of the stage.

WOMAN   How you feeling?
        You okay?

MAN   The investigation report came back

WOMAN   What report?

MAN   About Wonderland

WOMAN   And?

MAN   They let me go

WOMAN   They fired you?

MAN   Yes

Woman goes to man.

MAN   I don't want to talk about it

Woman stops.

On the other side of the stage.

SON   Then sometimes
                    He'll talk
                              about his wife
                                        Maybe he'll talk
                              about his children
                                        about his work
                                   Or he'll talk
                    about his boyfriend
               Suddenly
                    this stranger thinks
               I'm an old friend buddy pal from way back when
                    He'll tell you
               his dreams
                    his fantasies
                              his fears
          like I'm some $200 shrink
               But
                    I listen
                         'cause I'm supposed to

He's the gentle one
                  There are others
              Harder
          Rougher
          Who'll hurt you
                      in cars
              in dark street corners
                      in an alley someplace

Son kneels on the floor. Son slams his hand on the ground, making a sound.

On the other side of the stage, responding to the sound, Man suddenly bolts toward the window.

MAN Listen
         Did you—?

WOMAN What—?

MAN I thought I—

WOMAN Not again—

MAN But I—

WOMAN A noise—

MAN Yes I—

WOMAN No—

MAN This time—
         I—

WOMAN He's not coming back
           He will never come back
           We chase him out

chase him away
He will never come home

On the other side of the stage. Son lies on a bed.

SON   But if I'm lucky
                I'll find myself in some HoJo
                    some Holiday Inn
                            some Motel Six
                        where it's a little warmer
            where I can take a hot shower
                            watch a little TV
                lie in a soft bed

                        Meanwhile
                the angel
            his fingers
                    they run
                        fumble
                    pry into
            my shirt my jeans my underwear

                I close my eyes
            and I don't think anymore
                I just see
                    in my mind's eye
                        That golden carpet

            And this time
                I don't wait
                            don't hesitate
                'Stead
                    I run

                    run far
                        run free

On the other side of the stage. Man and Woman in bed. Woman
looks at sleeping Man.

WOMAN   In the middle of the night
                   I stare at him
                   across the big big bed
                   He on one side
                   I on the other

                   For a moment
                   I wonder
                   if everything is real
                   This bed
                   This man
                   This room
                   This house
                   This life

                   This son
                   My son

                   Suddenly
                   he turn over
                   his face toward mine
                   his eyes shut
                   his breathing gentle

                   Then
                   his hand
                   as if by instinct
                   find mine

And he hold onto it
My hand
A perfect fit

And I realize
it's real
I'm real
He's real

Everything is real

Sound of traffic.

YOUNG MAN   The Man
                        he runs around Downtown Los Angeles
                                Hollywood
                                        Silverlake—

MAN   Have you?—

YOUNG MAN   Holding firm
                        a picture photograph of the son
                                he tries to undo his wrong—

MAN   Have you seen my son?—

YOUNG MAN   He takes to countless nameless streets
                                stopping bystanders
                        asking strangers
                                if they have seen a runaway son—

MAN   Excuse me
        Have you?—

YOUNG MAN   In response
                        the man receives a litany
                                        of blank faces
                                blank stares—

MAN   Please—

YOUNG MAN   On the western end of Los Angeles
                        the Woman
          she carries a brown box
                        Xeroxed canary-yellow fliers
                                    posters of a missing son
          she ferociously litters them in her wake—

WOMAN   Ay
          You see him?—

YOUNG MAN   She posts them on shop windows
                        post offices
                                    lampposts—

WOMAN   You see him
          my son?—

YOUNG MAN   She goes to
                        churches community centers gay bars
                She walks into
          city morgues city hospitals city shelters
                        looking
                                    begging for any clue
                                                any information
                that may lead her to her son prodigal—

WOMAN   He not black hair anymore
          He blond
          Marilyn Monroe blond—

YOUNG MAN   After a day of pounding the pavement
                        the Man
                with a brown bottle
                        in a brown paper bag

staggers back
into the cold embrace of the mall

In a scant sea of oblivious shoppers
he sits quietly
unseen and unheard
sipping from a bottle of golden brown scotch
in a dark corner of the food court

MAN   And no matter how far
how far I run
I end up
here
in Wonderland

I spend
most of my days
these days
nowadays
here
I stay here
until it's time
time to go home

I like it
here
It's quiet
comfortable
and
and
oh
so dark
It shelters me
from the blinding light
light outside

(Beat)

> You know what's funny?
> I don't really
> think
> think about the sixteen
> sixteen people
> at all
>
> The sixteen
> sixteen innocents
> I killed
> buried in the mall
>
> I know I'm supposed to
> I try to
> think about them
> I want to
> think about them
> but I don't
> I can't

(Laughs)

> At the end of the day
> you count your blessings
>
> You play the game
> by the rules
> You listen to God
> His rules
>
> And
> You have nothing
>
> Not even a son
>
> My son

Young Man looks at Man.

YOUNG MAN   All the could'ves
               All the should'ves
                   A little too late
                       Dad
                   A little too late

(Sound of park traffic)

                 Cross town
          In the concrete jungle gray of the city
   A hiccup of unexpected green
                     A park

        And in front of a black black pond
     we see her
          sitting aimlessly
                on an empty park bench
       in the dying sunlight
                   of a late afternoon

WOMAN   I come here
      every week
      to county museum

      After Rodin statue
      I sit right here
      La Brea Tar Pit

      Take bus
      RTD
      One and half hours to get here
      Can you believe?
      Faster to wait for menopause

      Something draw me here
      The fiberglass imperial mammoth

Right over there
See?
Three of them
imperial mammoth
Fancy Latin name for elephant

They fascinate me
The interesting thing is
they are like family
The father mammoth
stand there
expressionless
with the son mammoth
on the land
The father look helpless
The son lifting the trunk
braying braying braying
very touching
Can almost see tears

The mother mammoth?
Sure you can guess
There
In the tar
Half sinking in there
She knows
Shit
Too late

What I don't understand is
Why is woman elephant sinking
and not man?
How can father and son mammoth
just stand there?

How can anyone see
their mother in last dying moment
screaming screaming for help
and do nothing?

Instead
They stand
Gawk
See mother sink
Disappear
Plop
into black tar
become mineral rich
more fuel for RTD bus

But I think
this is prehistoric lesson
for woman daughters and mothers
about husbands sons and fathers

So I come here
every week
every Thursday
to pay respect
to mother mammoth

Because I think
I understand

YOUNG MAN   The Woman
                she sits there
                          sits there and sits there
          until the sun drowns
                in the tar black sky

                     Nightfall

Sound of street traffic.

YOUNG MAN   Thunder

        It's raining
           Hollywood Boulevard
      The Man
          he walks heavily on the wet stars of
                Bette Davis
             Clark Gable
              Lana Turner

          Suddenly
        he stops
     in front of the Lumiere
      a familiar movie theater
   where many summers ago
 the Man and his Son spent a lifetime
     basking in the glow of
           its oh so bright marquee
          its Technicolor movies

      Head tipped
           the Man stares
    blinks hard
      a paper slip
       a tip
    an address
      to his runaway son

     After a moment
              he enters—

MAN   I enter the dark stuffy theater
In almost perfect unison
several heads turn

swivel
Quickly
I find a seat near me

Then
a spiraling drumroll
The moment everyone's waiting for
A harsh spotlight
It floods the stage
announcing it's show time

(*Son enters dancing.*)

There he is
With a winning all-American
clean-scrubbed
boy-next-door smile
He coquettishly skips
to the front of the stage
Smile dance flash
In a cowboy costume
sequined in red white and blue
Bare chest
he toys with his oversized Stetson
Kicking his boots
This dancer
This boy
This son
My son

My son
he smiles dances flashes
There
To a hand
emerging

from the horizon of dark seats
promising a dollar bill
He is the star of the show
The main attraction
And he knows it

I close my eyes
close them shut
close them tight
till it hurts
When I pry them open again
He's gone
He is back stage

Should I see him?
What will I say?
Will he come home?
Will he just come home and be my son again?
Like he's supposed to
And everything will be all right again

I see
in the corner of my eye
several men
getting up
heading to a dark room

But
I don't
I can't follow them in

Instead
I run
on the crimson-carpeted aisle
I part

the theater doors open
I slip out
into the oncoming symphony
of street traffic

I merge
I drown
I disappear

Man walks away.

SON Sure
   I knew it was him
    It had to be
   Even in silhouette
      It's the way he sits
    that slouch
       His posture
       his size

    I recognized his scent immediately
   His barbershop Vitalis
     sharp
       distinct
       sweet

   Even in the dark
      when he's saying nothing
  how could you not recognize
       your own father?

    So Dad
      you wanna see how I operate?
    Wanna see how I turn tricks?
Wanna see how I'm doing without your help?
      Without your dollar bills?

                    Wanna see?
                          Wanna see?
                                Huh?

(*Beat*)

            I couldn't run after him
                  I wanted to

                        But I couldn't
            Just couldn't

(*Beat*)

                        Instead I wondered
            what I'd wear for tomorrow's audition

Sound of film studio traffic.

YOUNG MAN   Cross fade
                        Cross town
                  Chatter chatter buzz buzz
                        of people running up and down
      Makeup people
            camera crew
                  lighting grips
                  A Hollywood soundstage

            A film shoot is about to get underway

SON   "Well, one must be serious about something,
      if one wants to have any amusement in life"

                        Well what do you think?
                  Not bad huh?
                        No it's not from a movie
            Oscar Wilde

The Importance of Being Earnest
No
I don't know if it's on video

(*A strong and harsh spotlight hits Son.*)

Wow
The lights
It's bright
Man
Bright
and hot
Hey is that a camera?
Man
Like real Hollywood stuff
Do I have a script or—
No script
Just what?
Improvise
Ad lib

No shit
Stallone
he started out this way too?

Hey
if Stallone can do it
so can I
And look where he ended up
You gotta see the big picture

I know what I'm getting into and—
I'm not some punk idiot that—
Besides I'm not going to do this forever 'cause—
This is my big break and—

So you want me to what?
                Come into the apartment
                        Speak broken English
                Deliver Thai food
                        So I'm the take-out guy
                Right?
                        Cool

        He is wearing a what?
                        A bathrobe
                He exits to get money
                                I see magazines
                        on the table
                Dirty magazines
                        I get aroused
Okay that is an intention I can work with

        He comes back in
                        this time
                                without
                                        the bathrobe
                        looks at me
                        He smiles
                Says I look Cambodian Vietnamese something
I say we all look alike
                He's a Vietnam vet
He asks if I ever watched *The Killing Fields*?
                I say yes
        It was exactly like my life

                He gets aroused
                        comforts me
                                touches me

                                        Cool

Then flashback

We're in a jungle
it's raining
there are napalm bombs going off everywhere
and it's romantic
He pretends to be an American soldier
I pretend to be a Vietcong pilot
He captures me
on suspicion of spying
tries to break my spirit
'stead he breaks me in

Then after having sex with him
Because I feel tremendous love for him
And yet at the same time
Conflicted
Disloyal to Ho Chi Minh and my country
I disembowel myself with a large samurai sword

Okay

I see Spielberg written all over it
Sure
Oscar stuff
Really
Hey
listen
You got some christine
X special K coke smack
or something
I need some
to get going
Morning glory?
Love to have some

427

                                        Yeah
                        before we get rolling
                                Great
                        Gimme some man

                                                Yeah
        Easy does it
                Great
                        Great
                                Hits the spot
                Wow
                        Yeah
                                Out of this world
                        Out of this
                                Out

                                        Out
                                                Yeah
                        What?
                                        Yeah
                I'm ready
                        Sure
                I'm ready
                                Ready
                        Yeah

                I'm a survivor
                        A survivor
                                Survivor

        YOUNG MAN   Out
                A makeshift sound stage in Encino

                        Out
                An endless maze of city streets

                                428

                    Out
        A vast network of endless arteries
                            endless veins
            of endless people and traffic
                flowing
                        coursing
                            pulsating

                                    Silence

            A secluded world of green
                        A college campus

        We see
            the face of the Man

Sound of lecture hall noises.

YOUNG MAN   Given   **MAN**   The function of
            the dire   most buildings is
            financial straits   to protect people
        he is swimming in   from the weather
                Given   by creating
    his new found celebrity   enclosed but
        the Man   interconnected
        he agrees   spaces
to go on a lecture circuit   The structural
            in colleges   components
    universities   of a building
        architectural   assure that the
                schools   elements required
            to make   to fulfill
        ends meet   its function
                                     to stand up

Sound of applause.

429

MAN Thank you all
for inviting me here
to speak today on
"Why Buildings Fall"

We'll take questions from the audience

Young Man assumes the role of a college student. He raises his hand.

MAN Yes—

YOUNG MAN So you were found guilty
of negligence—

MAN Yes—

YOUNG MAN And your architectural license
was stripped away from you?—

MAN Yes—

YOUNG MAN And the victims' families are intending
to sue you in civil court—?

MAN Yes—

YOUNG MAN What do you with your spare time?
I mean
you spent your entire life
as an architect
drawing drafting designing
and then
one morning you wake up
and you realize you can't do it anymore
not like you don't have the know-how
or the talent or the skill
but they won't let you do it

How does that make you feel?

Silence.

MAN   Thank you again for your time—

YOUNG MAN   No
             Wait
                  I asked you a question
                           How do you feel—?

MAN   Another appointment
           Pomona College
           to speak on—

YOUNG MAN   How do you feel?

Beat.

MAN   How do I feel?

           All your lifelong dreams
           all your lifelong drawings
           will remain permanently on paper
           Buildings
           that will never see the light of day
           Buildings
           that will never reach
           touch the heavens

           Because you need the money
           you sell yourself
           to buildings
           of higher learning
           There you tell younger versions of yourself
           again
           again
           and again
           the familiar tale of what you did wrong

and not
the story of the man you were meant to be

Man walks away.

Sound of ocean.

YOUNG MAN　From another day
of brightening
educating the young minds of America
the Man goes home

And guess who
he sees standing in the front door?—
Liz Taylor
in *Who's Afraid of Virginia Woolf?*

WOMAN　Today
some policemen
come by house
put paper on door
A notice from the sheriff's department

What is it?

Eviction notice
ordering us to vacate
premises in a month

What?
How did this—
I cannot believe—
This is our home
My home
We live here
more than twenty years

Must count for something
right?

Now they want to take my home
Foreclosure they say
Procedure they say
Sorry they say
To me
just another piece of a paper

We default on payments
mortgage payments?

How come you never tell me?
How come we default?
How long we default?

No money
Where are savings?
No savings
I cannot believe
You said we have—
What do you mean
We have nothing?

Nothing
We have nothing
Not a cent
Everything we have
on credit
Everything
on credit
Car
House
Furniture

TV
Clothes
Everything
All we have
all borrowed
all on credit
Now no house
What to do?

Ay
Tell me
Tell me
Why you just stand there?
Keep quiet
All you do
stand there in the balcony
looking at the ocean
staring

There is nothing there
nothing
no golden carpet
no nothing

Ay
Are you listening?

*Man continues to look out into the ocean. Woman stares at Man.
Both stand silently.*

YOUNG MAN   Up
                    Gently
                        to the clear
                            expansive
                                endless

                              azure sky

                                    Embrace the sky

                                          Hold

                              Down

                        Slowly

                                    It's a month later—

WOMAN   So what we do now?

MAN   I don't know

WOMAN   They say
         they come tomorrow

         Tomorrow

Long silence.

MAN   I have been thinking—
       Maybe we can go back
       back to Singapore—

WOMAN   Go back to Singapore
         for what?—

MAN   To start all over again
       From the beginning—

WOMAN   Why?

MAN   Remember what fun we had?—

WOMAN   What are you talking about?—
         "Remember remember"—

MAN   How we made love—
       Remember how happy we were—

WOMAN Stop this nonsense—!

MAN How we first started out—
What dreams
what plans both of us—

WOMAN That is long time ago—

MAN You wanted to be a salesgirl for Macy's
and I wanted to be—

WOMAN Now is different—

MAN Maybe we can move there—

WOMAN You cannot go back—

MAN Move to Singapore and—

WOMAN This here is home—

MAN Start all over again—

WOMAN Now we have no home—

MAN Let's go—

WOMAN We have nothing—

MAN Let's leave—

WOMAN What's wrong with you?

MAN We can leave tomorrow—

WOMAN We have nothing

We have nothing

Do you hear me?

Nothing

Nothing

Nothing

Woman stares at Man.

Pause.

Woman runs off.

Silence.

Man looks at the ocean.

Sound of a roar of plane taking off.

YOUNG MAN   A screaming sky
                The deafening howl of jet planes

            Los Angeles International Airport

WOMAN   I arrive in airport

Young Man assumes the role of the immigration officer.

        I walk to white man
        in immigration counter
        I say
        "I want to go home"

        He smile
        He say
        "Sorry honey
        You can't board aircraft
        without a ticket"

        I say
        "I come from Singapore
        I want to go back
        Have to go back"

He smile
He say
"I'm afraid I can't help you
Little lady
You live here now
in America"

All of sudden
I remember this man
I think he forget me
I think he same person
Same person who let me into America

I say
"Hey mister
You remember me?
I come here
many many years ago
You let me in"

He smile
He say
He doesn't remember
He let a lot of my type in here every day

I get desperate
I say
"Please sir please I have nowhere to—
My house all gone—
I need to go back—
Need to go home
Please let me
Please
Let me
go home"

I hear him
mumble to the security guards
"First you can't keep them out
now you can't keep them in
Wish they'd make up their goddamn minds"

But I don't hear anymore
All I want is to go home
Go back home
and all that is blocking me
is this immigration officer fool

So when he doesn't look
I run
run into departure lounge
where passengers all boarding airplane
leaving for Singapore

I hear
Shout
"Stop! Stop!"

(Joyously)

So I run
Run far
Run free

Behind me
security guards running

But I faster than them
I sprint into the gate
disappear

I see the airplane
in front of me

But before I reach airplane door
they grab me
pin me to the ground

(*Woman falls to the ground.*)

I scream!
"Let go! Let go! Let go!"
I beg!
I plead!
I have to get on plane!
Have to get home!
But they don't hear!
Don't hear me!

Then
suddenly
I
give
up
Tired
I stop

"Sorry
Don't know what happened
I just want to go back to Singapore
I'm homesick
I'm okay now
Sorry
Don't know why I act like this
Will go home now
Will go home now"

Sound of ocean.

YOUNG MAN It's late afternoon—

Young Man sees Man entering.

YOUNG MAN Back at the Sandpiper—

> Dad—

> > He—

> > > He—

Silence.

MAN You need to take care
of a wife
a son
and a place to call home

So you sign
Your life
on the dotted line

This is the right thing to do

The right thing

Man runs to the edge of the stage.

MAN I run
run far
run free

Out of the house
Into the streets
I continue my run
until I reach
the water's edge

(*Beat*)

And there
I see
the golden carpet
God has once again
unfolded in front of me

An invisible voice
it tells me
leave everything behind
escape
run to the great beyond

This time
I don't wait
don't hesitate

Instead
I run
run far
run free

(*Man smiles and raises his hands.*)

I'm home

Sound of ocean.

WOMAN   After airport
I come back to house
sit on balcony
and look out into ocean

I sit there for long time
Suddenly I see
I see him
there

over there

My husband

(Sound of ocean getting louder and it builds to a startling crescendo at the end of the scene)

He stand
near the water
looking out

Then
I see him
He walk
slowly
into ocean
not looking back

I want to
say
say something
Shout
but cannot
cannot
say anything

I see him
waist deep
in water
fighting
strong waves

Determined
he keep on
walking deliberately
into ocean

I know what he's doing
but I
cannot
don't want to
stop him

So I just
look
stare

Suddenly

Big wave
Crash
So loud

Ocean
Swallow him up

And he
He disappear
Vanish
Gone

(*Silence*)

Don't know why

I cannot

cannot

cannot

stop him

Sound of ocean roaring very loudly.

YOUNG MAN   With a slight breeze
          blowing on her face
    The Woman
           She stands
                alone
                    tall
                silhouetted by the glittering
                    blinding
                setting sun

    The ocean
        in the near distance
                pound pound pounding on the rocks
Music music music

        Fade to black

        The end

     So what do you think?
        My first attempt at a screenplay and—
                I call it *A Beautiful Country*
        It's a working title—
        If you don't like it—
                I'm not—

        Too ethnic?
             Hey, no problem—
I can make them white—
             Limited appeal?—
    Too down?—
                Not high concept enough?—
Hey I can see where you're coming from—
        I can nix the man walking into the ocean—

Maybe give it a happier ending—
I see—
Too small—

No no I can't see Stallone playing the father

(*Silence*)

Well
George
Glad you could take time out
to hear my pitch
Hey
Seems everything's going great for you
Career
Marriage
Children
A new house in the hills
Who'd have thought, you know?

It's great seeing you again
after all these years
I was just thinking
when we were kids?
Remember how we used to rehearse
Oscar Wilde
after school?

Yeah
Those were the days

My Dad?
Nope
Didn't go to his funeral
Read about it in the newspapers though

446

I haven't seen my mom in years
I just know she's—
It's been years

(*Silence*)

Listen
I better run
Yeah
Got to prep for tomorrow's shoot

No
No scripts
No lines
All improv
All ad lib

It's a job

(*Young Man turns to go but stops.*)

You know what's weird, George?
This screenwriting stuff is—
It's like what my dad used to do
as an architect

There is a kinda—
Magic—
to it

First there's nothing
but space
Blank space
Emptiness

Then Dad
he would draw a line
One line

And another

        And another

              Next thing you know

You got a building

      a city

A country

A world

          It's so unreal

The funny thing is

      now I think I understand what my dad saw

              in a blank piece of paper

      a white sheet of nothing

      Except it's not nothing

It's a million possibilities

      A million realities

Like a million shining stars

      in a dark dark night

          That's what he saw

I don't why I wanted to tell you that

      I just thought you'd want to know

Sound of ocean.

Woman is sitting on a bench. She is dressed like a homeless woman.

Young Man enters and sees Woman.

YOUNG MAN Mom?
    Is that you?
      Why are you dressed like—

WOMAN Why you here?

YOUNG MAN I'm just passing through

WOMAN Really

YOUNG MAN I come by the house
                                        sometimes

WOMAN Why?

YOUNG MAN Just to visit

WOMAN Homesick

YOUNG MAN Maybe

Silence.

YOUNG MAN Mom
   Are you all right?
                  Do you need—?

WOMAN Your father

YOUNG MAN I know

WOMAN He plop
            Died
            A year ago

YOUNG MAN Yes
   Saw it on TV newspapers

Silence.

Woman takes out a crumpled piece of paper.

WOMAN You see this?

YOUNG MAN What is it?

Young Man takes paper from Woman.

WOMAN Insurance

Woman suddenly laughs.

449

WOMAN After he plop
some men
in three-piece suit
come by house
They say
they cannot honor premium
only for accident
acts of God
not for swimming in ocean
This paper
worth hundred of thousands
now
worth nothing

You know
your father
he love you
very much

YOUNG MAN I know

Silence.

Woman looks out into the ocean.

WOMAN Hmm
Quiet
Calm
It's lonely here

Beat.

YOUNG MAN "It's lonely here
Like we were the only two people left in the
whole world—"

WOMAN "Maybe we are—"

YOUNG MAN "Maybe when we get back to shore—"

WOMAN "Everyone else would have disappeared—"

YOUNG MAN "I'd like that, wouldn't you?"

WOMAN *A Place in the Sun*

YOUNG MAN Elizabeth Taylor

WOMAN Actually Shelley Winters
Before she plop
into water

YOUNG MAN Really

WOMAN Really

Woman and Young Man laugh softly.

YOUNG MAN Where are you staying?

WOMAN In Wonderland

YOUNG MAN In the mall?

WOMAN Yes

Mall very empty now
Business very bad
Lots of shops vacant
and no security guard

So at night
I slip in
sleep on bench

It's safe

YOUNG MAN You know
Mom

                    you can come stay with me
                              It's a small place but—

WOMAN   No
            Thank you
            I'm okay
            Really

            Staying there
            feel like
            staying closer to him
            Your father

            I'm happy

(*Beat.*)

WOMAN   Are you happy?

YOUNG MAN   Yeah
                    I'm happy

                         I'm doing okay
                              doing what I like

                    Did a couple of films—

WOMAN   So you are success
            Movie star
            Like Montgomery Clift—

YOUNG MAN   I guess

(*Woman sits down.*)

YOUNG MAN   What are you doing here?

WOMAN   Watching ocean

(*Pause*)

WOMAN Sometimes I look
look at ocean
And if I look hard enough
I think
I see Singapore

(*Woman laughs.*)

YOUNG MAN Can I sit with you?

WOMAN If you like

Beat.

YOUNG MAN Dad used to say
He'd look out and wait

WOMAN Wait for what?

Man appears.

MAN That—

YOUNG MAN That—

WOMAN What?—

MAN There—

YOUNG MAN There—

Son appears.

MAN Over there—

SON Over there—

YOUNG MAN The golden carpet—

WOMAN Golden carpet—

YOUNG MAN There—

SON There—

MAN   Can you see it?—

YOUNG MAN   Can you?—

Woman looks out sadly.

WOMAN   Yes

       Yes

       I can see

       I can see

Sound of ocean.

The lights fade to black.

THE END